PL'

present

# BAD JAZZ
## By Robert Farquhar

**The first performance of Bad Jazz took place on Thursday 22nd February 2007 at the Drum Theatre Plymouth.**

## Cast

| | |
|---|---|
| Natasha | Leah Muller |
| Ben | Alex Palmer |
| Gavin | Louis Hilyer |
| Danny | Neil Stuke |
| Hannah | Pia de Keyser |
| Danielle | Laura Macaulay |
| Ewan | Alan Tripney |

## Creative Team

| | |
|---|---|
| Director | Gordon Anderson |
| Designer | Soutra Gilmour |
| Lighting Designer | Tim Mascall |
| Music | Ben Hales |
| Casting Director | Julia Horan |
| Fight Director | Philip d'Orléans |
| Company Stage Manager | Marius Rønning |
| Technical Stage Manager | Anthony Newton |

## For ATC

| | |
|---|---|
| Executive Producer | Emma Dunton |
| Administrator | Kendall O'Neill |
| Graphic Design | Mark Goddard |

## For Drum Theatre Plymouth

| | |
|---|---|
| Production Manager | Nick Soper |
| Costume Supervisor | Lorna Greenwood |
| Sets, props and costumes | TR2 – Theatre Royal Plymouth Production Centre |

## BIOGRAPHIES

### Gordon Anderson – Director
Gordon is Artistic Director of ATC. He also directs *The Catherine Tate Show* for Tiger Aspect/BBC2 and *Suburban Shootout* for Feelgood Fiction/Channel 5. He has directed productions for some of the country's leading companies including: the Royal Court Theatre, Bristol Old Vic, Lyric Hammersmith, Manchester Royal Exchange, English Touring Opera and Scottish Opera.

### Pia de Keyser – Hannah
Trained: Central School of Speech and Drama. Theatre includes: *The French Lieutenants Woman* (Nick Brooke Productions, No 1 Tour), *Jane Eyre* (Shared Experience, West End), *Newsrevue, Newsrevue Christmas Special* (Canal Café Theatre), *The Second Generation* (Royal Court). Television includes: *Holby City* (BBC). Radio includes: *Orwell's Babies* (BBC Radio 4). Voice Over includes: *Twisted TV 15X30* (Challenge TV). *Interactive Video, Habla Ingles?* (Ocean Video).

### Emma Dunton – Executive Producer
Since joining ATC in 2001 Emma has produced *Gizmo Love* by John Kolvenbach, *A Brief History of Helen of Troy* by Mark Schultz, *Jeff Koons* by Rainald Goetz, *Country Music* and *One Minute* by Simon Stephens, *Excuses!* by Joan Joel and Jordi Sanchez, *Out of Our Heads* by Susan Earl and Janice Phayre, *Arabian Night* by Roland Schimmelpfennig and *In the Solitude of Cotton-Fields* by Bernard-Marie Koltes. At Volcano Theatre Company she produced and managed the national and international tours of *Macbeth-Director's Cut, The Town That Went Mad* and *Private Lives*. Previously she has worked at the British Council and on feature films in Los Angeles.

### Robert Farquhar – Writer
Robert's plays include *Dead Heavy Fantastic, Empty the Thought Bubble, Kissing Sid James, Almost Forever But, God's Official, Dust to Dust*, and *You Are Here*. They have been performed at theatres all over the UK and Internationally, including Liverpool Everyman, West Yorkshire Playhouse, Hull Truck, Botton Octagon and Edinburgh Assembly Rooms. He recently directed and scripted *Insomnobabble* for Big WoW, and is under commission to the Liverpool Everyman.

## Soutra Gilmour – Designer

Theatre Includes: *The Caretaker* (Sheffield Theatre), *Shadow of A Boy* (RNT), *Country Music* (Royal Court), *Hair* (The Gate), *Ghost City* (59E59 New York), *When The World Was Green* (Young Vic), *Life Begins Season 04* (Liverpool Everyman), *Through The Leaves* (The Duchess Theatre), *The Woman Who Swallowed A Pin* (Southwark Playhouse), *Therese Raquin* (Citizens Theatre, Glasgow), *Hand In Hand* (Hampstead), *The Birthday Party* (Crucible, Sheffield), *Witness* (The Gate), *Tear From A Glass Eye* (The Gate/National Studio). Opera Includes: *Mary Stuart* (ETO), *Girl of Sand* (The Almeida), *El Cimmaron* (QEH), *La Boheme* (Opera Ireland), *A Better Place* (ENO), *Eight Songs For A Mad King* (World Tour), *Saul, Hansel and Gretal* (Opera North) and *Mahlers Ruckert Lieder* (Streetwise Opera). Upcoming work includes *Angels in America* (Lyric Hammersmith).

## Ben Hales – Music

Ben Hales is a musician and songwriter. He has toured extensively with various bands since abandoning a drama degree at Goldsmiths College in 1993. In 2002 he began working as a freelance songwriter and signed to SonyBMG Music Publishing in 2005. He has written songs and performed with numerous artists including Aqualung, Duke Special and Melanie Blatt (All Saints). Production music credits include soundtracks for commercials for Mitsubishi and Wrigley's and original music for theatre including ATC's *Gizmo Love, Splendid Productions, Resistible Rise of Arturo Ui* and *Antigone*. He is currently co-producing Aqualung's third album for Columbia Records.

## Louis Hilyer – Gavin

Theatre includes: *King Lear* (RSC), *The Tempest* (Old Vic Theatre), *A Russian in the Woods* (RSC), *The Taming of the Shrew* (RSC), *An Inspector Calls* (RNT). Television includes: *The Ten Commandments, Lewis, The Verdict, Armadillo.* Film includes: *Modigliani.*

## Julia Horan CDG – Casting Director

Recent theatre credits include: *Dying for It* (Almeida), *pool (no water)* (Frantic Assembly), *Rabbit* (Old Red Lion), *Gaddafi - A Living Myth* (ENO), *A Brief History of Helen of Troy* (ATC), *The Prayer Room* (Birmingham Rep/EIF), *As You Like It* (Wyndhams), *One Under* (Tricycle), *Anna in the Tropics* (Hampstead), *Othello* (Cheek by Jowl), *The Soldiers' Fortune, Tintin, The Skin of our Teeth, Hobson's Choice, The Daughter-in-law, Homebody Kabul, A Raisin in the Sun, Six Characters Looking for an Author,* (Young Vic), *The Morris, Port Authority, Urban Legend, The Kindness of Strangers, Yellowman* (Liverpool Everyman), *The Girl on the*

*Sofa* (EIF/Schaubuhne Theatre, Berlin), *Original Sin* (Crucible, Sheffield), *Antarctica* (Savoy), *The Weir* (Duke of York's), *The Force of Change, Made of Stone, Local, Trade, About a Boy, Yardgal, Holy Mothers, Last Dance at Dum-Dum* (Royal Court). Television includes: *The Verdict* (BBC2/RDF).

### Laura Macaulay – Danielle
Laura trained in New York at HB Studios with Uta Hagen and at The Neighborhood Playhouse School of the Theater with Sanford Meisner. Theatre includes: *Cancer Tales* (Wolsey, Ipswich), *Can't Stand Up For Falling Down* (Bridewell), *The Guardsman* (Albery, West End), *Strike Gently, Away From Body* (Young Vic), *Clubbed Out* (Royal Court), *The Measles* (The Gate, London), *Schoolgirls In Uniform* (BAC), *The Shift* (Young Vic), *The Ladies Of The Corridor* (Finborough). Television includes: *Blessed* (BBC), *Hollyoaks* (C4), *Family Affairs* (C5), *High Stakes, Series II* ( LWT), *As If,* (C4), *My Family* (BBC), *Norman Ormal* (C4), *The Regicides* (C4), *The Badness Of King George IV* (C4), *A Likeness In Stone* (BBC). Film includes: *Virtual Sexuality* (Columbia Tri Star Pictures), *Comic Act* (Spider Pictures). Radio includes: *Woof Woof Woof* (BBC Radio 4), *The Scuffed Shoe* (BBC Radio 2).

### Tim Mascall – Lighting Designer
Recent lighting design credits include (London and West End) *Derren Brown – Something Wicked This Way Comes* (Old Vic) *The Pool* (Arts Theatre) *Breakfast With Jonny Wilkinson* (Menier Chocolate Factory) *Lies Have Been Told – An Evening With Robert Maxwell* (Trafalgar Studios) *Behind The Iron Mask* (Duchess Theatre), *The Vagina Monologues* (Wyndams Theatre), *The Road To Nirvana* (Kings Head) *Why The Whales Came* (Comedy Theatre), *Professor Bernhardi' and 'Rose Bernd* (Arcola Theatre), *Vote Dizzy* (Soho Theatre), *Filler Up* (Drill Hall), *ZooNation Dance* (Sadlers Wells), *When Harry Met Barry* (workshop production at The Venue). National Tours include: *Gizmo Love* for ATC and *Trainspotting* for MGL. Tim has also work internationally on operas and theatre in Australia, America, Italy, Canada and Germany.

### Leah Muller – Natasha
Theatre includes: *IWitness* (Finborough Theatre), *pool (no water)* (Frantic Assembly/Lyric Hammersmith), *The Romans in Britain* (Crucible Theatre Sheffield), *The Tempest* (Liverpool Playhouse), *The Crucible* (Birmingham Rep/Centreline), *Paradise Lost* (Royal Theatre Northampton), *Tops Girls* (Manchester Library Theatre), *The Girl on the Sofa* (Edinburgh International Festival/Shaubuhne Theater, Berlin), *The Seagull* (Royal Northampton Theatres), *Emma* (Haymarket Theatre Basingstoke ), *The Frankenstein Project* (National Theatre Studio), *Hayfever* (Oxford Stage

Company), *Six Characters Looking for an Author* (Olivier Award Nominee, Young Vic), *Arms & the Man, The Captain's Tiger, The House of Bernarda Alba* (Richmond Orange Tree Theatre). Television includes: *Man & Boy* (BBC, Simon Curtis), *The Bill* (Pearson/Thames Television, Mike Cocker), *Casualty* (BBC, Michael Morris). Film includes: *A Touch of Sadness* and *Vagabond Shoes* (Ugly Duckling Productions, Jackie Udney). Opera includes: *The Trojans* (ENO, Richard Jones).

### Anthony Newton – Technical Stage Manager
Anthony graduated from QMUC, Edinburgh in 2004. After university, he worked as a designer for 18 months in an event lighting company before pursuing a career in theatre as a freelance lighting designer, production manager and technician. His work includes designs for Southwark Playhouse, Stephen Joseph Youth Theatre and Cat In A Cup and relights on an international tour for Universal Arts. Most recently he was TSM for Graeae.

### Kendall O'Neill – Administrator
Kendall joined ATC in April 2006. Originally from Chicago, Kendall spent the last three years working in New York. She was the assistant director on Mark Schultz's *A Brief History of Helen of Troy* at Soho Rep. Kendall has also worked for Manhattan Theatre Club, Williamstown Theatre Festival and The Flea Theatre. Most recently Kendall was the assistant director on Daniel Kramer's production of *Woyzeck* at St. Ann's Warehouse in Brooklyn.

### Alex Palmer – Ben
Theatre includes: *About the Boy* (Royal Court), *The Novice* (Richard Eyre), *Blood Red Saffron Yellow* (Plymouth Theatre Royal). Film includes: *Harry Potter & the Goblet of Fire* (Warner Bros, Mike Newell), *Master and Commander Far Side of the World* (20th Century Fox, Peter Weir), *28 Days Later* (Danny Boyle), *Still Crazy, Closing the Ring* (Sir Richard Attenborough). Television includes: *Doc Martin* (ITV, Ben Bolt), *Spooks* (BBC Television, Ciaran Donnelly), *Innocents* (Peter Kosminsky), *Armadillo, Butterfly Collectors, Night Flight, Walking with Cavemen, Mrs Bradley Mysteries, Who Killed Charlie Bravo, The Iceman Murder.*

### Marius Rønning – Company Stage Manager
Marius has been working as a freelancer since 2001. He has worked for Trestle (Mask), Tete a Tete (Opera), Royal College of Music (Opera), New Kent Opera, English Touring Opera, Wee (Dance), Soho Theatre, the Royal Court Theatre, Tamasha, Graeae and ATC. This is Marius' fifth show with ATC.

**Neil Stuke – Danny**
Theatre includes: *A Night at the Dogs* (Soho Theatre), *Blue/Orange* (Duchess), *Threesome* (Lyric Hammersmith), *Entertaining Mr. Sloane* (Arts Theatre), *The Bullet* (Donmar Warehouse), *Featuring Loretta* (Hampstead), *Grace Note* (Old Vic), *American Buffalo* (Young Vic), *Clocks and Whistles* (Bush Theatre), *Mojo* (Royal Court), *What the Butler Saw* (The Royal Exchange), *Goldhawk Road* (Bush Theatre). Film includes: *Out on a Limb, Mother Theresa, School for Seduction, Christy Malry's Own Double Entry, Circus, If Only, Sliding Doors, Dead Bolt Dead.* Television includes: *The Bill-Year Long Guest Lead, The Catherine Tate Show, The Sins, Bedtime, Afternoon Play, Drop the Dead Donkey, Between the Lines, Chopra's Town, Elizabeth – The Virgin Queen, Sound Proof, Silent Witness, 20,000 Streets Under the Sky, Faith, Murphy's Law, Murder in Mind, Game On, Trust, Grafters.* Upcoming work includes *Kingdom* with Stephen Fry.

**Alan Tripney – Ewan**
Trained: RSAMD. Theatre includes: *The Matinee Idle* (Oran Mor Theatre, Liz Lochead), *My Old Man* (Magnetic North, Nicholas Bone), *If Destroyed True* (Paines Plough/Dundee Rep/Menier Chocolate Factory, John Tiffany), *Slab Boys, Cutting a Rug* (Traverse, Roxana Silbert and Phillip Howard). Television includes: *Feel the Force* (BBC2/Catherine Bailey Productions) and *Monarch of the Glen* (BBC/Ecosse).

ATC was founded in 1979 to tour innovative work throughout the UK. Over the years the company has developed a tradition of ensemble excellence and a reputation for originality and internationalism, picking up many awards along the way. Since Gordon Anderson and Emma Dunton joined the company in 2001 ATC has focused upon contemporary work and forged dynamic partnerships with companies and artists from across the world. All ATC productions are UK or world premieres.

In August 2006 ATC presented **Gizmo Love** by John Kolvenbach at the Edinburgh Festival.  Other recent touring productions include: **A Brief History of Helen of Troy** by Mark Schultz which was performed at Soho Theatre and was nominated for a TMA Award in the Best Touring Production catagory; **Jeff Koons** by German playwright Rainald Goetz which was performed at the Institute of Contemporary Arts; the Catalan comedy **Excuses!** by Joel Joan and Jordi Sanchez in co-production with Barcelona based theatre company Krampack; **Country Music** in co-production with the Royal Court Theatre and **One Minute** by award-winning British playwright Simon Stephens at the Bush Theatre; **Arabian Night** by Roland Schimmelpfennig; **Out of Our Heads** by comedy duo Susan & Janice; and Bernard Marie Koltes' **In the Solitude of Cotton Fields** in a site-specific production at the disused Aldwych Underground station on the Strand.

*'..Anderson's sensitive, precise direction has paid off brilliantly here…the meticulous acting is as persuasive as the direction.'*
– The Times (*One Minute*)

*'Really really incredible..intricately detailed..amazing..this is a remarkable American play..'* *****
– Time Out 'Critics Choice' (*A Brief History of Helen of Troy*)

**ATC, Malvern House, 15-16 Nassau Street, London W1W 7AB**
**T: 020 7580 7723, F: 020 7580 7724**
**E: atc@atc-online.com**
**www.atc-online.com**

ATC is funded by the Arts Council England

# Drum Theatre Plymouth

The Drum Theatre Plymouth has become a driving force in the South West and beyond, pioneering new forms of stage writing, physical theatre and other innovative work. As part of the Theatre Royal Plymouth complex, it has taken a leading role in an ongoing national exploration of new ways of producing and seeing theatre. In both 2002 and 2005 the Drum Theatre was nominated for the prestigious Peter Brook Empty Space Award.

The Theatre Royal's Young Company and People's Company have residency in the Drum Theatre, which also hosts extensive community and participation work. The Drum includes in its programme a network of leading national theatre companies – Graeae Theatre Company, ATC, Royal Court, Suspect Culture, Paines Plough, Half Moon, Red Shift Theatre Company, Travelling Light Theatre Company and Kesselofski and Fiske.

The Theatre Royal Plymouth is made up of the Theatre Royal itself and the Drum Theatre, as well as TR2, a new, innovative and award-winning Production and Education Centre housing the theatre-making processes, rehearsal facilities and extensive education, access and development activities.

**Recent productions:**

| | |
|---|---|
| July 2004 | The Owl Service<br>adapted by Anita Sullivan and David Prescott<br>from the novel by Alan Garner<br>Producer: Drum Theatre Plymouth |
| September 2004 | The Wonderful World of Dissocia<br>by Anthony Nielson<br>Producers: Drum Theatre Plymouth, Edinburgh<br>International Festival, Tron Theatre, Glasgow |
| October 2004 | Through a Cloud<br>by Jack Shepherd<br>Producers: Drum Theatre Plymouth and<br>Birmingham Rep |

| | |
|---|---|
| February 2005 | Mercury Fur<br>by Philip Ridley<br>Producers: Drum Theatre Plymouth and Paines Plough |
| May 2005 | Stoning Mary<br>by Debbie Tucker Green<br>Producers: Drum Theatre Plymouth and Royal Court |
| September 2005 | A Brief History of Helen of Troy<br>by Mark Schultz<br>Producers: Drum Theatre Plymouth and ATC |
| October 2005 | Presence<br>by Doug Lucie<br>Producer: Drum Theatre Plymouth |
| February 2006 | The Escapologist<br>by Simon Bent<br>Producers: Drum Theatre Plymouth, Suspect Culture and Tramway |
| May 2006 | NHS – The Musical<br>By Nick Stimson and Jimmy Jewell<br>Producer: Drum Theatre Plymouth |
| June 2006 | Pricked<br>by Anita Sullivan<br>Producers: Drum Theatre Plymouth and Ripple |
| September 2006 | pool (no water)<br>by Mark Ravenhill<br>Producers: Drum Theatre Plymouth, Frantic Assembly and Lyric Hammersmith |
| October 2006 | Long Time Dead<br>by Rona Munro<br>Producers: Drum Theatre Plymouth and Paines Plough |
| February 2007 | Bad Jazz<br>By Robert Farquhar<br>Producers: Drum Theatre Plymouth and ATC |

**DRUM THEATRE PLYMOUTH**
**Royal Parade, Plymouth, PL1 2TR**
**01752 267222**
**www.theatreroyal.com**

# BAD JAZZ

by Robert Farquhar

## JOSEF WEINBERGER PLAYS

LONDON

For Stephen Willems, who rescued an interesting mess.
Also with thanks to Trip Cullman.


"And though she feels as if she's in a play,
She is anyway."   *The Beatles*

# CHARACTERS

BEN

NATASHA

DANNY

GAVIN

HANNAH

DANIELLE

EWAN

## Scene One

*Natasha and Ben. He is dressed in shirt and tie, dull office style. She is waiting for a response.*

NATASHA          So?

                 (BEN *doesn't say anything.*)

NATASHA          Say something.

                 (BEN *still doesn't say anything.*)

NATASHA          Ben?

BEN              What?

NATASHA          I want to know what you think.

BEN              What did you say?

NATASHA          When?

BEN              What do you mean, when? When whoever it was, who, when it was suggested Tash, because, who did suggest it?

NATASHA          Why do you want to know that?

BEN              I don't know, maybe I'm a bit weird, but –

NATASHA          Gavin.

BEN              Gavin? It was Gavin's idea?

NATASHA          Yes, I suppose so, yes.

BEN              Right, so, in the middle of the tea break, he went, oh yea, by the way, I was thinking that instead of –

NATASHA          No, of course he didn't.

BEN              So, how then?

NATASHA      It wasn't like that at all.

BEN      And what did Danny have to say?

NATASHA      I'm not sure, I can't remember.

BEN      You're can't remember? Bloody hell, Tash.

NATASHA      Ben, you might not think it, but I do understand, that, how, potentially, for you, this is probably not an easy thing to deal with.

BEN      But what did he say?

NATASHA      Look, whatever Danny said, I don't think, because, Gavin, he is such, he's an inspirational director, and I know he –

BEN      Oh yes, Gavin the inspi-fucking-rational, I wondered how long it was going to be before we heard that one.

NATASHA      Ben please, this is not helping.

BEN      Oh, I am so sorry.

NATASHA      I want us to discuss this, and –

BEN      I didn't realise I was supposed to be being helpful.

NATASHA      And if you just stopped, reacting, every time I try to explain something.

BEN      Okay, okay, alright, let me get this straight. It has been suggested –

NATASHA      Suggested, yes.

BEN      By Gavin?

NATASHA      Yes.

BEN      That, in the play, there is now going to be this, moment.

| | |
|---|---|
| NATASHA | This is uncompromising stuff, Ben. |
| BEN | I do know that, Tash. |
| NATASHA | This isn't some light, comic farce. |
| BEN | Sure, okay, I understand all that. |
| NATASHA | And you did read it. |
| BEN | I know, but I didn't think – |
| NATASHA | We sat just here, and we talked about it. |
| BEN | Okay, yes, but I didn't think – |
| NATASHA | You didn't think what? |
| BEN | I didn't think that when I read the stage direction 'she performs oral sex' that meant you were actually, actually, going to be performing a, real, fucking blowjob, for real, in a play, on stage, in front of a paying audience. I might have this wrong, but normally, that bit where it says you suck another man's penis, that, normally, that doesn't actually really happen. |
| | (*Silence.*) |
| NATASHA | It's a play, Ben. |
| BEN | I know it's a play. |
| NATASHA | It's not real. |
| BEN | What? |
| NATASHA | I don't mean that, I mean – |
| BEN | How much more real do you want it to get? |
| NATASHA | We are talking about one moment, that would last, thirty, forty seconds. |
| BEN | Whoa, hold on, you've timed it? |

NATASHA       No, all I'm saying is, you have to consider it in the, the context of the whole play.

BEN       Oh, of course.

NATASHA       Because then, rather than it –

BEN       It all makes sense now, the context of the whole play, of course, oh yea, thanks for the insight, Tash, because –

NATASHA       Why do you always treat me like this?

BEN       Eh?

NATASHA       You always do that, you always make out I'm stupid, that, intellectually, I'm somehow beneath you.

BEN       When did I say you were stupid?

NATASHA       You imply it.

BEN       I do not.

NATASHA       That is so often the subtext.

BEN       Naïve, maybe.

NATASHA       I am not naïve.

BEN       You are naïve, come on.

NATASHA       See, you always do that, you try and pigeonhole me.

BEN       It's not a pigeonhole, it's a character trait.

NATASHA       Naïve is just stupid, but using a different word.

BEN       Okay then, what if I was Danny?

NATASHA       What? Why are you saying that?

BEN       Say, I was in a play, and –

| | |
|---|---|
| NATASHA | I thought you were giving up acting. |
| BEN | (*mimics*) 'I thought you were giving up acting.' |
| NATASHA | What? What is that? |
| BEN | (*luvvie*) 'Because I'm an actor, you know.' |
| NATASHA | Ben, fuck off, that's out of order. |
| BEN | But what would you say if just because I haven't given up – |
| NATASHA | Just because I haven't gone and got a job in an office somewhere – |
| BEN | Yes alright – |
| NATASHA | Just because I still think that one day, I might actually be able to, to say I'm an actress, and not feel as though I'm some sort of fake. |
| BEN | Okay, but what about, what about if it was part of some, away day, training, thing? |
| NATASHA | What was? |
| BEN | A trust exercise. |
| NATASHA | What are you talking about? |
| BEN | And they say, yea, it's a bit radical this, but run with it, but what we would like you to do, is for you, Ben, and you, Liz – |
| NATASHA | Who's Liz? |
| BEN | I don't know, I've just made her up. |
| NATASHA | What? |
| BEN | Purely in the interests of oiling the wheels of social intercourse. |
| NATASHA | Will you stop this. |

BEN          What we would really like you to do is –

NATASHA      Ben.

BEN          Is for you, Liz, to sit on Ben's face.

             (*Beat.*)

BEN          What would you say?

NATASHA      This is pointless.

BEN          What would be your thoughts on that
             particular scenario?

             (*They start to overrun.*)

NATASHA      This isn't so easy for me, you know.

BEN          What would you say?

NATASHA      I wouldn't say anything because it's so
             pathetic.

BEN          But what would you say? Go on, just, imagine,
             what would you say? What? For example? Shall
             I give you a choice of the sort of things you
             might potentially respond with?

NATASHA      Did you not hear what I said? No. I'm not
             playing this game. No. Ben. No. Stop it. Stop it.
             I said . . .

BEN          Come on.

NATASHA      No!

             (*Silence.*)

NATASHA      There was that French-Canadian piece last
             year. Do you remember it?

BEN          No.

NATASHA      It was in that disused warehouse, you had to
             meet up near London Bridge, and then they
             took you there, and –

BEN            What about it?

NATASHA        There was a scene in that where, one of the
               actors, he, he ejaculated.

BEN            He did, what?

NATASHA        Simone went to see it.

BEN            Every night?

NATASHA        No, she didn't go every night.

BEN            No, I mean, the actor, you're telling me that,
               every night, he, actually, every night . . .

NATASHA        He's an actor Ben, yes, of course. Yes.

               (BEN *is speechless.*)

NATASHA        And Simone said, she said, it was very
               beautiful.

BEN            Did she?

NATASHA        Because, the actor, he was playing, his
               character was dying.

BEN            Oh dear. What of?

NATASHA        Cancer, something terminal, I'm not sure, but it
               was set in the, the thirties I think. Before the
               war, and, the story it was, this particular scene
               was in a hospital, it was visually breathtaking
               apparently, but, in this scene, the, the man was
               dying, and there was a nurse, and she was
               washing him, and there was all this other stuff,
               her marriage was in crisis, and he'd written
               this, brilliant unpublished novel, and, anyway,
               because she was in love with him, and they
               both know he's dying, and this moment is
               probably, they know that this is probably the
               last ever time he's going to be able to, get an

erection, and so, she, because she loves him,
she . . .

(*Silence.*)

NATASHA        And Simone said it was beautiful.


Scene Two

*The rehearsal room.* NATASHA *and* DANNY *are in the middle of
rehearsing the play.* BEN *has literally just stumbled into the
space, uninvited, and unannounced. He is very drunk, and a
mess. His nose is bleeding. Also present are* GAVIN, *director,
and* HANNAH, *playwright.*

BEN            Tash!

NATASHA        Ben, what are you doing?

               (BEN *moves further into the room.*)

GAVIN          Who the hell, what is this?

NATASHA        What are you doing here?

BEN            Please Tash, we need to talk.

GAVIN          Who the fuck, we're in the middle of a
               rehearsal, who is this?

NATASHA        I'm sorry Gavin, I'm so sorry.

BEN            Tash, please, I've been thinking about
               everything, and –

NATASHA        Ben, you're drunk, go away.

BEN            We need to talk.

NATASHA        And you're bleeding. What have you been
               doing?

BEN            And then everything can be like it was.

NATASHA        No, Ben, not now.

| | |
|---|---|
| GAVIN | What is this? |
| BEN | I'm in pain Tash, I'm suffering. |
| GAVIN | Look, will somebody tell me what . . . |
| BEN | We have to talk, I have to explain to you what I've been thinking. |

(BEN *walks further into the room. He knocks over a chair.*)

| | |
|---|---|
| GAVIN | Ah, no. No, no, no, that's, hey, enough. |
| NATASHA | Ben! What do you think you're doing? |
| BEN | Please Tash, look, I'm sorry, I just want to talk to Tash, that's all, please. |

(BEN *has started to tug at* NATASHA. *Everybody is now shouting.*)

| | |
|---|---|
| GAVIN | Hey, hey, oi, leave her alone. |
| BEN | Please, a few minutes, that's all, please. |
| DANNY | Look, don't do that, I don't think you should be doing that. |
| GAVIN | Oi. Stop that. Oi. Jesus Christ. |
| BEN | Please, Tash, please. |
| NATASHA | Ben, no, you can't do this, stop it, stop it, get off me, Ben! |
| BEN | There's someting I have to say. |

(*Everybody stands back.*)

| | |
|---|---|
| GAVIN | Okay. |
| BEN | Listen to me Tash, please, I've been thinking about everything, us, the last few days, that's |

all I've been doing, and, I know what, listen to
me, I've got it all worked out, please. Okay, this
is it, this is it . . .

(BEN *tries to make his big speech. Nothing
happens.*)

BEN        Shit. Shit.

GAVIN      Okay, that's it. You need to leave.

BEN        It was up here, I had it all worked out.

GAVIN      Do you hear me?

NATASHA    This is not fair, Ben.

           (BEN *is madly trying to remember what it was.*)

GAVIN      I want you to leave.

BEN        Oh, Christ, shit. Just give a minute.

DANNY      Come on, Ben mate, I think maybe what . . .

           (DANNY *touches* BEN *on the arm.*)

BEN        Hey, hey, do not fucking touch me.

DANNY      Sorry.

BEN        And don't be calling me mate.

GAVIN      Okay, enough.

BEN        I am so not your mate, mate.

GAVIN      I want you out.

NATASHA    Ben.

GAVIN      Do I have to literally make you do that?

NATASHA    Please, Ben.

BEN        I don't want you to do the play, Tash.

| | |
|---|---|
| NATASHA | What? No. |
| GAVIN | I don't believe this. |
| BEN | Because if you do, I might do something. |
| | (*Beat.*) |
| BEN | I'm not saying I would, but I might, I can't promise. |
| GAVIN | Fuck's sake. |
| | (HANNAH *is writing something down in her notebook.* BEN *sees her doing this.*) |
| BEN | What's she doing? |
| GAVIN | Look . . . |
| BEN | She just wrote something down. She was looking at me, and then, I saw her, she wrote something in that book. |
| NATASHA | Ben . . . |
| BEN | What did you write down? |
| GAVIN | I'm really losing my fucking patience here. |
| BEN | I saw her, excuse me, excuse me, but what did you just write down? |
| HANNAH | Nothing. |
| BEN | Don't lie to me. |
| GAVIN | Oi. |
| HANNAH | It was just a thought I had, an idea. |
| NATASHA | Leave her alone, Ben. |
| BEN | I saw her, she wrote something down about me, she's sitting there scribbling down ideas that exploit my pain for her creative ends. |

GAVIN       She can write down whatever she wants.

HANNAH      It was only two words.

BEN         But I have a right to know what those two
            words were.

GAVIN       No, you don't.

            (BEN *lunges towards* HANNAH *in an attempt to
            grab the notebook. Chaos. Everybody is
            shouting.*)

GAVIN       Hey. Oi. Leave her alone.

NATASHA     Ben, stop this. Please.

BEN         Give me that notebook. You can't do this.

HANNAH      Get off, you maniac.

DANNY       Are you alright, Hannah?

            (*Chaos builds. Expand verbiage to fit the
            moment.* GAVIN *has hold of* BEN. BEN *throws
            him off.*)

BEN         Fucking get off me!

            (*Everybody steps back.*)

GAVIN       That's it, I'm getting somebody up here.

HANNAH      You assaulted me.

BEN         No, I didn't assault you, I just want to see what
            you wrote about me.

NATASHA     You lunged at her, Ben.

BEN         No, no, I was lunging for the notebook.

GAVIN       Is that what you want me to do? Call the
            police?

| | |
|---|---|
| BEN | Come on Tash, this is me, I don't go round assaulting playwrights. |
| GAVIN | Did you hear me? |
| BEN | Four years Tash, surely that must mean something. |
| GAVIN | Oi. |
| BEN | Look, I just want to talk to Tash. |
| GAVIN | Well she doesn't want to talk to you. |
| BEN | Oh, you really think you're something, don't you? |
| GAVIN | What? |
| BEN | Mister, creative, fucking, genius, and all his, fucking, actors doing whatever he says. |
| GAVIN | What is this? |
| NATASHA | Ben! |
| BEN | I love you Tash. |
| NATASHA | What? Don't say that. |
| BEN | But I do, I love you. |
| NATASHA | No. |
| BEN | What's wrong with that? I love you, I love you Tash. |
| GAVIN | No, no, no. |
| BEN | Let's get married. |
| NATASHA | What? |
| BEN | What do you say? Let's go off somewhere. Now. Las Vegas. Let's just do it, come on, get on a plane, and get married. Yea? Just, fucking, go, and, and . . . |

| | |
|---|---|
| NATASHA | Stop this, Ben. |
| BEN | Fuck the play. |
| NATASHA | No. |
| BEN | Fuck the play, because I love you, Tash. |
| NATASHA | I can't do that. |
| BEN | I'm bleeding, I love you so much. |
| NATASHA | But Ben, Ben. |
| BEN | I love you, do you hear what I'm saying, I love you. |
| NATASHA | I don't love you. |
| | (*Silence.*) |
| | That thing that was us, it's, finished. It's dead. |
| BEN | No. |
| NATASHA | Yes. I'm doing the play. |
| | (BEN *looks at everyone, and then starts to leave.* HANNAH *writes something in her notebook.*) |
| BEN | What's she doing? |
| GAVIN | None of your business. |
| BEN | I saw her, I turned to leave, and she wrote something down. |
| GAVIN | Look . . . |
| BEN | She can't do that. |
| | (BEN *lunges for the notebook again. Chaos, noise, disruption.*) |

BEN            I want that notebook. Give me the, fucking,
               notebook. I don't want my life turned into some
               arty play.

               (*A struggle. Very messy.* NATASHA *is screaming.*
               DANNY *is trying to mediate.* GAVIN *has* BEN *in a
               headlock of some sort.* BEN *bites* GAVIN'S *hand.*
               GAVIN *punches* BEN *in the stomach. Effective.
               People out of breath.* HANNAH *picks up her
               notebook.*)


                         Scene Three

*The rehearsal room.* NATASHA *and* DANNY *are rehearsing the
play written by* HANNAH. GAVIN *and* HANNAH *sit watching them.
The actors are holding the scripts, although they sort of know
their lines. In the scene,* DANNY'S *character has unexpectedly
turned up at where* NATASHA'S *character lives.* NATASHA *is
obviously herself in something of a dangerous mood.*

GAVIN          Okay.

               (*They start the scene.*)

NATASHA        'What do you want?'

DANNY          'I wanted to see you.'

NATASHA        'Why?'

DANNY          'I thought we should, you know, like have a
               talk.'

               (*She says nothing.*)

DANNY          'I got you some flowers.'

NATASHA        'You can't just turn up here like this.'

DANNY          'They're for you. They're a present.'

NATASHA        'I don't want to see you. Go away.'

DANNY          'But what about the other night?'

NATASHA        'What about it?'

DANNY          'I thought it was special.'

NATASHA        'Special? How?'

DANNY          'You know, intimate. Special.'

NATASHA        'I was a cunt for your prick. What was so
               special about that?'

DANNY          'Don't say that.'

NATASHA        'That's all I am, a cunt for men to shove their
               pricks into.'

DANNY          'No that's not true.'

NATASHA        'A cunt, a prick, a whore, and a junkie. That's
               us.'

               (GAVIN *shifts in his chair.*)

DANNY          Sorry, did you –

GAVIN          Stay with it.

DANNY          I thought you were going to say something.

GAVIN          Keep going.

NATASHA        'I was a cunt for your prick. What was so
               special about that?'

DANNY          Er . . .

NATASHA        'I was a cunt for your prick. What was so
               special about that?'

DANNY          'Don't say that.'

NATASHA        'That's all I am, a cunt for men to shove their
               pricks into.'

DANNY          'No, that's not true.'

| | |
|---|---|
| NATASHA | 'A cunt, a prick, a whore, and a junkie. That's us.' |
| DANNY | 'No.' |
| NATASHA | 'You put your prick in my cunt, that's all.' |
| DANNY | 'But you said you loved me?' |
| NATASHA | 'It was a fuck. That's all it was, because me and you, we're just two fucked-up no-hopers who got fucked up on fuck knows what, and we fucked, we fucked, we . . .' No. |

(NATASHA *breaks off, very frustrated with herself.*)

| | |
|---|---|
| DANNY | Are you alright? What's the matter? |
| NATASHA | I don't feel as though, I'm not getting it. |
| DANNY | No, Jesus, it was scary. It was great. |
| GAVIN | Do it again. Now. |

(*Beat.*)

| | |
|---|---|
| GAVIN | Now. |
| NATASHA | 'A cunt, a prick, a whore, and a junkie. That's us.' |
| DANNY | 'No.' |
| NATASHA | 'You put your prick in my cunt, that's all.' |
| DANNY | 'But you said you loved me?' |
| NATASHA | 'It was a fuck. That's all it was, because me and you, we're just two fucked-up no-hopers who got fucked up on fuck knows what, and we, we, we fucked!' Shit. |

(NATASHA *breaks off again.*)

DANNY          Tash?

               (NATASHA *lets out a yell of sheer frustration.*)

NATASHA        I don't know what I'm saying, it's just, noise,
               because why is she doing this, coming out with
               all this, because, why, why, I feel like I'm just,
               some, mad, headless, fucking banshee going on
               and on, with no idea why, what I'm, just going,
               bleurgh, bleurgh, bleurgh, you know, just
               words, and fucking, nonsense, and, it's
               rubbish, it's shit, I have no idea what I'm
               saying, it's just, crap. Crap. Sorry. Fuck.

               (*Silence.*)

NATASHA        Why is she so angry? Why? Why does she say
               all these terrible things? Because, you know,
               he loves her doesn't he, and, I mean, they've
               had a really good time haven't they, and now
               she's just being this bitch, it's like, why, why,
               why is she saying these things, because, does
               she love him, is, is that, why is she, I have no
               idea what is going on here, because, aargh.

               (*Silence.*)

DANNY          Shall we take ten minutes?

NATASHA        I do not fucking get it!

               (*Silence.*)

GAVIN          Who is she?

NATASHA        What?

GAVIN          Who is she?

NATASHA        I have no idea, that's what I'm saying.

GAVIN          Who is she?

NATASHA        She, she's a prostitute, she . . .

GAVIN      And?

NATASHA    I don't know, she . . .

GAVIN      What's she feeling?

NATASHA    Anger.

GAVIN      And?

NATASHA    Self-loathing.

GAVIN      And?

NATASHA    Fear.

GAVIN      Of what?

NATASHA    I don't know, of everything.

GAVIN      Of what?

NATASHA    Of, of, of, him, of saying . . .

GAVIN      What?

NATASHA    I don't know.

GAVIN      What?

NATASHA    I love you.

GAVIN      Why?

NATASHA    Because, she, I don't know.

GAVIN      Why?

NATASHA    She, she's scared that, that if . . .

GAVIN      What?

NATASHA    What might happen.

GAVIN      When?

NATASHA     When she says it.

GAVIN       Says what?

NATASHA     I love you.

GAVIN       Why?

NATASHA     Because, I don't know.

GAVIN       Why don't you know?

NATASHA     What?

GAVIN       Why don't you know?

NATASHA     Are you asking me or asking her?

GAVIN       Just answer the question.

NATASHA     I have no idea, that's what I'm saying, I don't know, I, I feel, nothing makes sense, I feel so lost and confused, about what, you, because, when you keep saying, I don't know, I don't know what, I don't know anything.

            (*Silence.*)

GAVIN       Okay. That's it. That's where she is.

NATASHA     But –

GAVIN       What?

NATASHA     You're saying, what, what are you saying?

GAVIN       I'm saying that's how she is, here, now, but, what is great, what is fundamentally heroic about this, person, this human being, is, she wants to smash through that part of her, the suburban soul that we all carry round with us, she wants to rip it out, and destroy it, and kill it. Annihilate it. Love? What the fuck is love? She's not interested in, love, love as the great romantic con trick, love as some sort of heart-numbing bullshit. She wants to feel something that is, human, and messy, and, ecstatic, and miserable, and fucked up. She wants to experience something that is made up of sex, and cruelty, and blood, and shit, and not some sentimental wank that has been invented to make us feel okay about ourselves.

(*Silence.*)

GAVIN    She can smell truth. She can't articulate it, but, she knows, she understands with every fibre of her intuition, that most of the human race are no more than glorified zombies, who never think of anything worth thinking, who never do anything worth doing, and what she wants, deep in her, what she's reaching for is something that goes beyond all that, something that is far greater than the mindless, mind-dead, mediocre, existence that we are sold to us as a life worth living.

(*Silence.*)

GAVIN    Because she knows that if she doesn't do that, she might as well die. Do you understand what I'm saying? Look at me, Tash. Do you understand what I'm saying?

(*Beat.*)

NATASHA    Yes.

GAVIN    Danny?

DANNY    What?

GAVIN    Do you understand what I'm saying?

DANNY    Absolutely. Totally fucking got it.

NATASHA    'I was a cunt for your prick . . .'

DANNY    So, can I just . . .

GAVIN       What?

DANNY       I just want to ask a question.

NATASHA     'I was a cunt for your prick –'

DANNY       Just a really, really quick question.

GAVIN       Give me that.

            (GAVIN *grabs* DANNY'S *script from him. He rips
            it up.* HANNAH *watches, horrified.*)

NATASHA     'I was a cunt for your prick. What was so
            special about that?'

DANNY       Shit.

NATASHA     'That's all I am, a cunt for men to shove their
            pricks into.'

DANNY       'No, no, that's not true.'

NATASHA     'A cunt, a prick, a whore, and a junkie. That's
            us.'

DANNY       'No.'

NATASHA     'You put your prick in my cunt, that's all.'

DANNY       'But you said you loved me?'

NATASHA     'It was a fuck. That's it all it was, because me
            and you, we're two fucked-up no-hopers, who
            got fucked up on fuck knows what, and we
            fucked.'

GAVIN       Again.

            (*Beat* .)

GAVIN       Again.

NATASHA     'It was a fuck. That's it all it was, because me
            and you, we're two fucked-up no-hopers, who

got fucked up on fuck knows what, and we
fucked.'

GAVIN    Again.

NATASHA    'It was a fuck. That's it all it was, because me
and you, we're two fucked-up no-hopers, who
got fucked up on fuck knows what, and we
fucked.'

GAVIN    Again.

NATASHA    'It was a fuck. That's all it was, because me and
you, we're two fucked-up no-hopers, who got
fucked up on fuck knows what, and we fucked.'

GAVIN    Again.

NATASHA    'It, was a fuck, we, that's all it was, me and
you, it was a fuck, that's all it was, because, me
and you, we're, because, it was a fuck, it was a,
it was, a . . .

(NATASHA *screams. Silence. Everybody waits to
see what will happen next. She starts
improvising. The actors can maybe improvise
slightly at this point as well, as long as they
hit the lines at the end of the scene.*)

NATASHA    You prick.

DANNY    What?

GAVIN    Go on.

NATASHA    A prick with a prick that you put up my cunt.

DANNY    Fucking hell, what?

NATASHA    You shoved your prick up my cunt until you
spunked.

DANNY    Jesus Christ.

NATASHA    You squirted your lot in my cunt.

DANNY         Hey, stop it.

NATASHA       Stop what?

DANNY         Why are you talking like this?

NATASHA       Because that's what happened.

DANNY         No, no, that's wrong, it's more than that.

NATASHA       A prick, and a cunt.

DANNY         I love you.

NATASHA       You love my cunt.

DANNY         What? No.

NATASHA       You don't love my cunt?

DANNY         What? Of course I do, but, what –

NATASHA       If you love me, you love my cunt.

DANNY         Okay, Jesus Christ, but –

NATASHA       You love my cunt.

DANNY         Okay, I love your cunt.

              (*Beat.*)

NATASHA       Tell it.

DANNY         What?

NATASHA       Get on your knees. Get down on your fucking
              knees, White Boy. On your knees.

              (DANNY *gets down on his knees.* NATASHA *sits
              in front of him, and spreads her legs.*)

NATASHA       Tell my cunt you love it.

              (*Beat.*)

DANNY          I love you.

NATASHA        I love you cunt.

DANNY          I love you cunt.

               (*A member of the audience walks out. Noisily.*
               GAVIN *turns to see that they've left. He turns*
               *back to* NATASHA *and* DANNY.)

GAVIN          Okay. Now we're starting to get somewhere.


                        Scene Four

*Very loud rock music.* NATASHA *and* DANNY *fall into the space.*
NATASHA'S *flat. They have obviously been drinking, and*
*probably a bit more. They are high on each other.* NATASHA
*hears something. Her mobile. She turns down the music.*

DANNY          Hey, what are you doing?

NATASHA        That's my phone.

DANNY          Leave it.

NATASHA        No, I want to know who's phoning me at this
               time of night.

DANNY          Come on, have you got any glasses?

NATASHA        I hate it when, ah.

               (*As she finds it, it stops ringing.*)

DANNY          And who was it?

NATASHA        Caller unknown.

DANNY          Okay, now is the time to get really fucking
               stupid.

               (DANNY *produces a bottle.*)

NATASHA        I bet it's Ben trying to spook me out.

DANNY          Well, fuck Ben, he's yesterday.

NATASHA        What?

DANNY          Come on, fuck him, phoning you at three in the
               morning, fuck him.

NATASHA        Yea, fuck him, fuck Ben.

DANNY          This is now.

NATASHA        Yea, fuck Ben.

DANNY          Fuck him.

NATASHA        Fuck him.

               (*They whip each other up, and then down the
               drinks* DANNY *has poured. They reel back from
               the hit. A moment where they catch each other,
               and realise what is about to happen.*)

DANNY          Nice space.

NATASHA        It's a bit minimal at the moment, you know,
               because . . .

DANNY          Hey, minimal is excellent, I love minimal.

NATASHA        So do I.

DANNY          Minimal is fucking great.

               (*They laugh.* NATASHA *is swaying to the music
               underneath.*)

DANNY          Christ. You are so . . .

NATASHA        What?

               (*Tension.* NATASHA *is enjoying it, though. She
               slightly poses for him.*)

DANNY          How much would you charge?

NATASHA     What?

DANNY       You know, like in the play. How much?

NATASHA     What are you talking about?

DANNY       Say, I was that sort of bloke, and I'd seen the
            advert, and rung up, and . . .

NATASHA     Danny?

DANNY       How much? Go on.

NATASHA     Are you seriously asking me?

DANNY       Yea, seriously.

NATASHA     No, get lost, I'm not answering that.

DANNY       You must have thought about it?

NATASHA     What?

DANNY       When you're not working.

NATASHA     Danny, in case you haven't noticed, I'm an
            actress.

DANNY       It's a lot better paid than waiting.

NATASHA     Er, yea, it probably is.

DANNY       Go on then.

NATASHA     No.

DANNY       Fuck me, you would make so much money.

NATASHA     Oh right, so you know about these sort of
            things do you?

DANNY       No, I'm just asking.

NATASHA     Are you enjoying this?

DANNY       Yea, but not as much as you.

NATASHA      Fuck off.

DANNY      How much?

NATASHA      No.

DANNY      Go on.

NATASHA      Danny, I'm not, no.

DANNY      How much? A rough guess, go on.

NATASHA      Alright, how much have you got?

     (*Beat.*)

NATASHA      Let's see the colour of your money, Danny boy.

     (DANNY *is very excited by this turn of events. He pulls out all his money. A pathetic bundle of notes and loose change.*)

NATASHA      What's that?

DANNY      That's all I've got.

NATASHA      I think I'm worth a bit more than that.

DANNY      What about a cheque?

NATASHA      I don't take cheques.

DANNY      Why not?

NATASHA      Because I don't.

     (NATASHA *is enjoying herself.*)

NATASHA      Oh dear, what's poor Danny going to do now?

     (DANNY *grabs his jacket, and starts madly searching through the pockets.*)

DANNY      Okay, look, hold on, hold on, hold on, okay, there you go.

(*He takes out an envelope, and produces from it, a substantial wad of money.*)

DANNY      Four hundred quid.

(*He puts the money down between them.*)

DANNY      It's my rent. I'm supposed to be paying it first thing tomorrow, but, the landlord, he lets us off a few quid if we pay cash.

(NATASHA *inspects the money. She looks at* DANNY.)

NATASHA    What service would you like?

DANNY      What, what service? Fuck, I like that, that's good, that's, Jesus, that's really . . .

NATASHA    Well?

DANNY      Er . . .

NATASHA    What would you like me to do for you?

(DANNY *takes a breath.*)

DANNY      Okay, what, what I would like you to, first of all, what I would like you to, to do is, oh man, is take off your knickers.

(*After a moment,* NATASHA *slips off her knickers.* DANNY *cannot believe what is happening.*)

DANNY      And then, I would, I'd very much appreciate it, if, if, if you sucked my penis.

(*They stare at each other.*)

NATASHA    And then?

DANNY      And then, after that, I, I would like you to tell me, that you love me.

(*Tension.*)

NATASHA          I think I can manage that.

(*A phone starts to ring, somewhere off. Getting louder. They don't move.*)


Scene Five

*The scene merges. Same time.* GAVIN *answers the phone that was ringing.* HANNAH.

GAVIN           Yes? Who is it?

(HANNAH *remains silent.*)

GAVIN           Oh, fuck this.

HANNAH          Gavin?

GAVIN           What, who is that?

HANNAH          Gavin.

GAVIN           Hannah? What's going on?

HANNAH          I'm sorry Gavin, I know it's late, but, sorry, did I get you out of bed?

GAVIN           Where are you?

HANNAH          I'm not sure.

GAVIN           Hannah, look, if this is like last time, you have to tell me.

HANNAH          I was in a taxi.

GAVIN           Okay, but –

HANNAH          And the taxi driver, he kept going on about the Chinese.

GAVIN           What?

| | |
|---|---|
| HANNAH | You know, about how in twenty years time, or even before that, they're going to be running the world, because there's so many of them. |
| GAVIN | So, after the taxi – |
| HANNAH | And do you know the first thing the world is going to run out of? |
| GAVIN | Please, Hannah. |
| HANNAH | Fluoride. |
| GAVIN | What? |
| HANNAH | Because of all the toothpaste. |
| GAVIN | Look, just – |
| HANNAH | And that is just so insane isn't it? We're living in this world as if nothing we do has any real consequence on anything, and that's just mad, I think the world's going mad Gavin, and nobody seems to have noticed. The world's fucked, it's really fucked. |
| GAVIN | I need to know where you are, Hannah. |
| HANNAH | Gavin? |
| GAVIN | What? |
| HANNAH | I want to talk about my play. |
| GAVIN | Okay. |
| HANNAH | It doesn't feel right. |
| GAVIN | What do you mean? |
| HANNAH | I feel as though, it's not my play anymore. |
| GAVIN | What did I say Hannah? |

| | |
|---|---|
| HANNAH | Yes, but I thought, I thought it would be different. |
| GAVIN | In what way? |
| HANNAH | I didn't think, when, because when I'm watching it, I didn't think it would be so, real, you know, it feels too real. |
| GAVIN | Look, Hannah. |
| HANNAH | Because the actors . . . |
| GAVIN | What about the actors? |
| HANNAH | When they say the lines, they don't sound like I thought they would sound when they were in my head. |

(*Somebody starts banging on the door in* HANNAH'S *background.*)

| | |
|---|---|
| HANNAH | Yes, okay. |
| GAVIN | What's that? |
| HANNAH | But my play, Gavin. |
| GAVIN | What was the banging, Hannah? |
| HANNAH | Why my play, Gavin? |
| GAVIN | Look, Hannah, what you have to realise is that, as a playwright – |
| HANNAH | Of all the plays in the world – |
| GAVIN | You are not the only author in the rehearsal room. |

(*The banging again.*)

| | |
|---|---|
| GAVIN | What the fuck is going on, Hannah? |
| HANNAH | Leave me alone. |

| GAVIN | Hannah? |
| HANNAH | I'll be out in a minute. |
| GAVIN | Who is banging on the door? |
| HANNAH | Can't we make it into a film? |
| GAVIN | What? |
| HANNAH | My play, we make it into a film, but when we show it, we say to people that it's a play. |
| GAVIN | Why would we do that? |
| HANNAH | Has that ever been done before? Alright, alright, alright. |
| GAVIN | Okay, you have to tell me where you are. |
| HANNAH | I don't feel so good. |
| GAVIN | What? |
| HANNAH | Okay, okay, stop banging. |
| GAVIN | What do you mean, you don't feel so good? |
| HANNAH | I think he wants to use his bathroom. |
| GAVIN | Who does? |
| HANNAH | The man banging on the door. |
| GAVIN | Who's the man banging on the door Hannah? |
| HANNAH | I think his name's Bob. |
| GAVIN | What are you doing in his bathroom Hannah? Hannah? What are you doing in his bathroom? |
|  | (*Beat.*) |
| HANNAH | That is quite a long story. |
| GAVIN | Fuck's sake. |

| | |
|---|---|
| HANNAH | I think he's very worried about me. |
| GAVIN | Why is he worried about you? |
| HANNAH | All I wanted to do was make some phone calls, and have a bit of lie down. |
| GAVIN | Hannah, I can't hear you, hold the phone nearer to your mouth. |

(*Rock music from previous starts up underneath. Banging on the door.*)

| | |
|---|---|
| HANNAH | How many aspirin would you say is too much? |
| GAVIN | Oh, Jesus. |
| HANNAH | I think I'm going to hang up now. |
| GAVIN | No. Hannah, don't . . . |

(*She hangs up.*)

| | |
|---|---|
| GAVIN | . . . hang up. |

(*Sound of disconnected phone, banging on door, rock music. Swells in volume and chaos. NATASHA and DANNY fucking. HANNAH collapsed. GAVIN. The soundscape morphs into 'bad jazz'.*)

## Scene Six

*The 'bad jazz' continues. An assault of noise and squeals. GAVIN, alone, in the rehearsal room. The music cuts out suddenly to a much more acceptable level. GAVIN is listening to the music on a portable CD player. He listens intently. NATASHA enters. GAVIN does not realise she is there. He begins to act out a scene, a moment, from something. This is the end of scene twelve. He experiments with volume levels. Talks to himself.*

| | |
|---|---|
| GAVIN | Louder. I want it louder. Louder. |

(*He stops the music. Silence.*)

NATASHA    Wow.

(GAVIN *turns.*)

NATASHA    Sorry, I, I didn't realise, because, I didn't mean
           to, because, you see, when I was at the tube, I
           realised I'd left my script behind, so, is that the
           music?

GAVIN      A few ideas.

NATASHA    God, that sounds amazing, I mean, like, really
           warped. Ah, there it is.

           (*She sees her script, and picks it up. She
           hovers for a moment, wanting to engage with
           GAVIN, but not sure how to.*)

GAVIN      Are you okay?

NATASHA    Am I, God, yea, I'm really, great. Absolutely.

           (*Beat.*)

NATASHA    I just feel, so, I don't know, just, everything at
           the moment, with the play, and everything,
           what we're doing, where you're forcing us to
           go with it, it's really, something, it's really, like
           this incredible journey, that, you don't know
           what's round the corner, it's amazing.

           (NATASHA *becomes embarrassed by her own
           enthusiasm.*)

NATASHA    Listen to me. That sounds really dim.

GAVIN      Don't put yourself down, Tash.

NATASHA    No, sorry, I'm always doing that.

GAVIN      You shouldn't underestimate yourself.

NATASHA    No, no, I won't. I'll try not to.

(*Beat.*)

GAVIN          So, you're off to see Hannah?

NATASHA        Yes, I am, tomorrow, when you and Danny are
               working on his speech. Her parents, they said,
               the morning is the best time to visit.

               (*Beat.*)

NATASHA        It's really strange her not being here isn't it.
               Not that she ever said a lot, but still, I
               suppose, you never know what's going on in
               somebody else's head, do you.

               (DANIELLE *enters. An officious quality to her.*)

DANIELLE       Gavin, I thought we were having a meeting?

GAVIN          I'm coming.

DANIELLE       Because there are quite a few things we need to
               talk about.

GAVIN          Okay.

DANIELLE       And I have something else I need to do.

GAVIN          I will be there when I've finished in here.

DANIELLE       Thank you.

               (DANIELLE *exits.* GAVIN *is obviously upset by
               this intrusion.* NATASHA *notices.*)

NATASHA        Are you okay?

GAVIN          Yea, I'm alright. It's nothing.

               (NATASHA *is not sure how to deal with* GAVIN'S
               *vulnerability.*)

NATASHA        I'll see you tomorrow then.

GAVIN          Maybe Hannah's doing the right thing.

| | |
|---|---|
| NATASHA | What? |
| GAVIN | Maybe, let the demons in, because, what's the alternative? |
| NATASHA | What do you mean? |
| GAVIN | Why not? Because, there has to be something else, than trying to please this, imaginary, fucking, average, focus group, demographic audience that supposedly exists somewhere, that everybody is so afraid of upsetting. |

(*Beat.*)

| | |
|---|---|
| GAVIN | That's where I went wrong. |
| NATASHA | What do you mean? |
| GAVIN | When I had my company, I thought I could change things, you know, by doing 'plays'. |
| NATASHA | But your production of, oh, where he has all the pockmarks . . . |
| GAVIN | 'The Changeling'. |
| NATASHA | My lecturer at college, I remember he said it was one of the most visceral experiences he's ever had in a theatre. |
| GAVIN | Yea, visceral, they liked saying that. |
| NATASHA | But surely . . . |
| GAVIN | It was okay. That's it. It was a bit more than a night out, but then the trouble was that was all ever wanted me to do again. The same old formula. Roll out another Jacobean tragedy. Or a Brecht. Or a Shakespeare. Or a Chekhov. But I wasn't interested. I wasn't interested in giving people what they think they want. One more radical reinterpretation of a classic. From the canon. I wasn't interested in signing up to be |

part of the great culture conspiracy, and
doffing my cap to the omniscient box-ticking
bureaucrats in the sky who giveth and taketh
away. Fuck that.

(*Beat.*)

GAVIN          Making people cry? Easy. Making people
laugh? Easy. Making people think they're
thinking? Easy. Make people come out of a
theatre, shaken, having to pick up the pieces of
what they thought they knew, to have their
psychic nervous systems ripped apart by
chaos, by noise, by poetry, beauty, unedited
electricity, now that is something worth
struggling for.

(NATASHA *is entranced.*)

GAVIN          Because who wants to be popular? Anybody
can be popular. Anybody can make some well-
meaning liberal stroke his beard, thinking he's
had his intellect stimulated, but what use is
that to anyone? Theatre, Natasha, theatre, must
always, always reserve the right to fuck over
people's minds.

(*Intense.*)

GAVIN          Do you understand what I'm saying?

(*Beat.*)

GAVIN          It's not a hobby, Natasha. Don't play at it.

(GAVIN *moves away.* NATASHA *is shaken.*)

GAVIN          I know this man, he's Greek, well, he's Greek-
Russian, but the thing is, this man is extremely
wealthy, and, he likes to consider himself, I
think you'd describe him as, a patron of the
starving artiste. And he happened to see some
of my work.

NATASHA        Was it . . .

GAVIN       Yes, and . . .

NATASHA     The Changeling?

GAVIN       Yes. And a few other things, but, as a result of
            this, me and him, we started having a dialogue.
            And he said to me, basically, he said he would
            provide the money for me to set up and run, a
            laboratory workshop. Funded by him.

NATASHA     Wow.

GAVIN       So, we looked around, saw quite a few places,
            and eventually, we found, this, factory, ex-
            factory in East Germany, or as was, and this
            factory, used to make ball-bearings, and it's in
            this small town, not too far from Berlin, but
            essentially, it's on its own, and it's there, some
            people might say the heating is not great, but
            we can sort that, and it's just sitting there, with
            all these, spaces, with this, atmosphere. It's
            perfect.

            (*Beat.*)

GAVIN       And sometime soon, and I mean soon, I'm
            going to handpick a group of actors, and I want
            us to go and live there, and work. Every day. A
            strict regime, exercises, physical training,
            emotional exploration. We'd improvise, tell
            stories, fuck about, invent, just constantly
            discover, constantly create new methods,
            metaphors, images, languages, anything,
            because we wouldn't have to pander to some
            commercial, knee-jerk, crowd-pleasing, bullshit.
            No. We'd be free of all that, it wouldn't be part
            of the landscape, because, if we wanted to, we
            could work on something for, two years, longer
            if necessary, and if we feel that it's not right, if
            it's not necessary, we don't have to cheapen
            ourselves by putting in front of an audience.
            We don't have to do it. The work is everything.

(*Silence.*)

NATASHA        That sounds incredible.

GAVIN          So, what do you think?

NATASHA        What do I think about what?

GAVIN          What do you think about being part of all that?

NATASHA        Me?

GAVIN          Yes, you. You, Natasha.

NATASHA        You mean, you, want me to go to Germany, and, do all that, work with you, and live, and, be there doing all, what you've just said?

GAVIN          You're willing to give yourself, Tash. And that's rare.

NATASHA        Oh my God, that's . . . I wasn't expecting, wow.

(NATASHA *pulls herself together slightly.*)

NATASHA        Of course. I think that sounds amazing.

(DANIELLE *enters.*)

DANIELLE       Gavin? I thought we said we were meeting.

(GAVIN *doesn't reply to this.*)

GAVIN          I will be there when I've finished here.

(DANIELLE *exits.*)

GAVIN          Think about it.

(GAVIN *starts to exit.*)

And Natasha, this is between us okay?

NATASHA        Of course. Yes. Okay.

(GAVIN *exits.* NATASHA, *alone. Bad jazz music. Suddenly too loud.*)

## Scene Seven

*Music cuts out. The rehearsal room. Following day.* DANNY
*sits, forlorn.* GAVIN *waits.*

DANNY          I'm sorry.

               (GAVIN *waits.*)

DANNY          Honestly, I was on top of it last night, I don't
               know what's going on, I'm really sorry.

GAVIN          For a start, you need to stop saying sorry.

DANNY          You're right, there's no point in, in, just
               getting all worked up, because, I know, I just
               have to get focused, and go for it. Yea. Just, do
               it.

               (*Beat.*)

DANNY          But if I could just take ten minutes?

GAVIN          Danny . . .

DANNY          I know, I know.

GAVIN          You should know this speech.

DANNY          I do know this speech.

GAVIN          Okay then.

DANNY          But it's just every time I go for it, I don't know,
               it's just like there's this little voice in my head,
               it's sitting there going, panic, panic, can't do
               it, must fuck it up.

GAVIN          Because if you don't know the speech . . .

DANNY          I do know the speech.

GAVIN        So, what is the problem then?

DANNY        Look, five minutes, get some fresh air.

GAVIN        No.

DANNY        Shit, you're right, I'm sorry.

GAVIN        And stop saying sorry.

DANNY        No, of course, I'm sorry, shit, I didn't mean to say that, shit, okay, okay, okay, I'm going go for it, I'm just going, fucking nail it. Yes.

             (DANNY *picks himself up, and launches into the speech.*)

DANNY        'The thing is, I don't feel right. My head, it's full of all this weird noise I can't get rid of. All these mad notes, and squeals, and screeches, it's like some sort of terrible music lodged in my brain. I feel as if I'm going insane.'

             (DANNY *struggles to find the next line.*)

DANNY        'I feel as if I'm going insane.'

             (*Still struggling, almost speaking to himself.*)

DANNY        'Mad notes, squeals, screeches, some sort of, of terrible music, lodged in my brain. I feel as if I'm, as if, I'm going insane.'

             (*He stops, thinks.*)

DANNY        'As if I'm going insane.'

             (*Beat.*)

DANNY        'I feel as if I'm going inane.'

             (*Beat.*)

DANNY        'I feel as if I'm going insane.'

| | |
|---|---|
| GAVIN | For crying out loud. |
| DANNY | Sorry. I'm sorry. I know you don't want me to say sorry, but fuck it, I'm saying it alright. Sorry. I'm, fucking, sorry. |

(DANNY *looks extremely defeated.*)

| | |
|---|---|
| GAVIN | This is not good, Danny. |
| DANNY | I know. |
| GAVIN | Frankly . . . |
| DANNY | I know. |
| GAVIN | This is . . . |
| DANNY | I know. |
| GAVIN | Fucking dreadful. |

(DANNY *hangs his head a bit lower. Close to tears.* GAVIN *waits.*)

DANNY          Do you mind if I, can I tell you something?

(GAVIN *waits.*)

DANNY          Natasha and me, we, we've been, seeing each
               other. Do you know what I'm saying? We,
               we've been, seeing a lot of each other, a lot,
               and, it's been amazing, and totally intense, but
               really weird as well because of the play, and
               Natasha, she didn't want you to know. She was
               very adamant about that. You mustn't tell
               Gavin, don't tell Gavin, but, fuck it, I've said it,
               I've told you, I mean, you probably knew
               anyway, but anyway. Anyway. So. Yesterday.
               No, day before yesterday, whenever it was, I
               get a phone call, totally out of the blue, from, a,
               an ex-girlfriend. Saskia. I don't know if you,
               you auditioned her once, long red hair, quite
               posh, you probably don't remember her, and
               anyway, she phoned me, and she said, she

wanted us to meet up, and, discuss, something,
but she couldn't say exactly what it was over
the phone, so, we, we arrange to meet in this
bar in Fulham. And, I was going to tell Tash, I
was, but, I don't know, there was, something,
in her voice, so I said I was just hooking up
with someone from drama school, which is not
strictly a lie, but, anyway, so I went, and
Saskia, she's there, and, I sit down, and, as
soon as I do that, she tells me, straight out, she
says, she is pregnant. And, I'm the father, no
way it could be anyone else, because, even
though we've been split up, like, nine months
now, we were still sleeping together up until,
well about two months ago, because, I don't
know, we just did, that's what happens isn't it,
and, so, I'm, a bit phased, a bit fuck me, that's,
I wasn't really expecting that, and she starts
saying all this stuff about how she's going to
keep it, you know, whatever I say, because
she's twenty-nine now, and not a lot is
happening for her acting-wise, and she reckons
this could be some big life change catalyst
thing for her, you know, being a mother, it
could really help her see what's really
important in life. And when she says that,
especially, the, being a mother, when she says
that, that's when, it's as if, this, fucking,
sledgehammer, just, it hits me, and my whole,
everything just goes, because, it's like my head
does this instant, mad, equation, you know,
Mother, Father, Mum, Dad, Dad, me, Dad
equals me, that means, I'm going to be
somebody's Dad, and when I think that, I start
laughing, not, ha ha that's funny laughing, I
mean really, a bit, do you know what I'm
saying, and Saskia, she joins in, and we're
sitting there, both of us, we're sitting there
laughing like two total maniacs, and then the
next thing I know, we're crying, and then we
start laughing again, and then we're crying,
and then we're laughing and crying at the same
time, and people are now openly staring at us,
and then Saskia says she's got some coke left

over from the weekend, and I mean, normally,
weekday, I wouldn't even contemplate it, but,
extraordinary circumstances, and all that, and
so we sneak off, and I'm thinking, hopefully
it's going to level me out, and we go for a walk,
and the sun is going down, and we go across
Battersea Bridge, and we go into the park, and
we wander round the Peace Pagoda, and we're
talking and talking about this miracle of
creating a new life, and how there's going to be
this, thing, that calls you Mum and Dad, you
know like your Mum and Dad, only this time,
it's you, not, and that is so fucking mind-
blowing, and then we find this club, and it's
heaving, and it's playing this, really,
absolutely mental hardcore headbanging shit,
and we just, dance, for hours, and hours, like,
total meltdown, and then, the next thing I know
is, we're back at Saskia's, and we're lying
there, naked, wrapped in an Indian rug for some
reason, and I can hear birdsong, and there's
light creeping in from somewhere, and, I don't
know, everything seemed so right, and so I
said to Saskia, I said, I asked her to marry me,
and she looked at me for a moment, but then
she goes, yes, and she starts crying, and she
phones her parents, and then her flatmate gets
up, and he cracks open this bottle of
champagne, and we drink this toast, you know,
to us, and the baby, as all this sunlight is
streaming into the room, and, and, that's it.
Yea. That's what I wanted to say. I'm getting
married. And I haven't told Natasha.

(*Silence.*)

GAVIN       Are you actually ever going to do this speech?

DANNY       Yea, of course, sorry, I . . .

GAVIN       The things is, Danny, can I remind you, we're
            making a play here.

DANNY       I know, sure, I totally believe in the play.

| | |
|---|---|
| GAVIN | This is what is important here. |
| DANNY | Of course. |
| GAVIN | Do you understand? |
| DANNY | Yes. |
| GAVIN | No, do you understand? |
| DANNY | Yes. I do. I understand. |
| | (*Beat.*) |
| GAVIN | Do the speech. |

### Scene Eight

GAVIN's *flat. A Scottish junkie rent boy. An awkwardness.*

| | |
|---|---|
| GAVIN | So, would you like something to drink? |
| EWAN | Have you got any pop? |
| GAVIN | Pop? You mean . . . |
| EWAN | Just, pop. You know, some fizzy pop. |
| GAVIN | No, no, I'm afraid I'm all out of pop. |
| EWAN | Aye, well, nay bother then. |
| | (*Beat.*) |
| GAVIN | So, do you have a name? |
| EWAN | Aye, I've got a name. |
| GAVIN | And what is it? |
| EWAN | Ewan. |
| GAVIN | Is that your real name? |

| | |
|---|---|
| EWAN | Of course it's my real name. Why, what's your real name? |

*(Beat.)*

| | |
|---|---|
| GAVIN | Danny. |
| EWAN | Danny? My old fellar was called Danny. Not that he's dead or anything, I just like to refer to him as though he is. |

*(Beat.)*

| | |
|---|---|
| EWAN | What do you do for a living then? |
| GAVIN | Why do you want to know that? |
| EWAN | I'm interested. You know, making conversation. |

*(GAVIN doesn't answer.)*

| | |
|---|---|
| EWAN | You're a bit arty, aren't you? |
| GAVIN | Am I? |
| EWAN | Aye, you've got a vibe. |

*(Beat.)*

| | |
|---|---|
| EWAN | Are you an actor? I reckon you're a fucking actor. |
| GAVIN | No, I'm not an actor. |
| EWAN | Well, you're not a painter are you? |
| GAVIN | No. |
| EWAN | Or one of them fellars who stands up there waving the wee stick thing. I used to have a regular who did that, and you're definitely not like him. |
| GAVIN | Look . . . |

| | |
|---|---|
| EWAN | Are you sure you're not an actor? |
| GAVIN | No. |
| EWAN | Because . . . |
| GAVIN | I'm a director. |
| EWAN | Okay, right, what, a film director? |
| GAVIN | No, theatre. I'm, a theatre director. |
| EWAN | Oh right, plays and that. You tell the actors where to stand, that sort of thing? |

(*Beat.*)

| | |
|---|---|
| EWAN | I always quite fancied that, being an actor. You know, being somebody else. It always had a certain appeal. Do you know what I'm saying? Hey, if you'd like me to suck your dick or anything, just give me the nod. |

(*Beat.*)

| | |
|---|---|
| EWAN | Because I was in a production of 'Joseph and his Technicolour Dream Coat' when I was at school. And I was Joseph. Aye, me. Get that. Andrew Lloyd-what's his face. |
| GAVIN | Webber. |
| EWAN | That's right. |
| GAVIN | And how was it? |
| EWAN | How was what? |
| GAVIN | The Lloyd-Webber experience. How did you rate it? |
| EWAN | Aye, well, it was great. I fucking loved it, you know, what with all the costumes, and backstage, and everybody clapping you at the end. It was a buzz. I felt like I was a somebody. |

GAVIN   A somebody?

EWAN    Aye, I felt famous.

GAVIN   That must have been something.

EWAN    It was, it was fucking great. I even signed some autographs.

GAVIN   And would you like to be famous?

EWAN    What, you mean . . .

GAVIN   Fame, Ewan, do you want it?

EWAN    Doesn't everybody?

GAVIN   But how much do you want it?

EWAN    Hey, what's with all the questions? Is this some sort of audition?

GAVIN   Let's see what you're made of.

EWAN    What are you fucking talking about?

GAVIN   What about a song?

        (*Beat.*)

EWAN    You what?

GAVIN   How's the voice these days?

EWAN    Hold on, are you, you want me to sing a song?

GAVIN   Have a go.

EWAN    What is this? Are you taking the piss?

GAVIN   Why not? One of the catchy ones.

EWAN    One of the what?

GAVIN   I'll count you in, one, two . . .

EWAN      Hey, oi, oi, let's get this straight mister, I do not do singing songs.

GAVIN      Come on.

EWAN      I haven't come up here to sing you a song.

GAVIN      Just a snatch of something.

EWAN      No, look, shall I not give your arse a bit of a tickle?

GAVIN      Something from 'Cats'? What about that?

EWAN      You what? 'Cats'? Are you for real?

GAVIN      Alright, what about the one with the roller skates?

EWAN      Fuck off.

GAVIN      Please, Ewan.

EWAN      This is really warped.

GAVIN      Entertain me, Ewan.

EWAN      You are one skewered bastard.

GAVIN      I would like to be entertained, Ewan

EWAN      Look, I'm a fucking rent boy, not Bruce Forsyth.

GAVIN      I want to escape the numbness of the everyday drudge.

EWAN      Okay, look, I was lying back there, my name isn't Ewan.

GAVIN      I want to forget who I am.

EWAN      Do you hear what I said? My name is Colin.

GAVIN      Give me some transcendent melodies, Ewan.

EWAN    What? You want some smack? Is that what you're saying?

GAVIN   No, Ewan, I want to hear you sing a song.

EWAN    I just said, my name isn't Ewan.

GAVIN   Come on, you know you want to.

EWAN    No.

GAVIN   Nobody else need know,

EWAN    I can't remember any of the fucking words.

GAVIN   Dig deep then, Ewan.

EWAN    Are you listening to what I'm saying here? I cannot . . .

GAVIN   All you have to do is believe in yourself, Ewan.

EWAN    Alright, that's fucking it, believe in yourself? I'm fucking out of here. And look, you can have your money back.

        (EWAN *fetches out a small handful of cash, and throws it at* GAVIN. *He turns to go.*)

GAVIN   You coward.

EWAN    What?

GAVIN   What a has-been.

EWAN    What are you saying?

GAVIN   He's bottled it. Can't live up to the hype.

EWAN    I don't fucking believe this.

GAVIN   For your mother, Ewan.

EWAN    Eh?

GAVIN        What about a wee little tune for your dear old
             mother, Ewan?

EWAN         My mother's dead, leave my mother out of this.

GAVIN        All the sweeter, Ewan.

EWAN         You are one sick bastard, do you know that?

GAVIN        Come on.

EWAN         Will you fuck off.

GAVIN        Sing for your supper, Ewan.

EWAN         And my name is not Ewan.

GAVIN        Sing.

EWAN         No.

GAVIN        This is your fifteen minutes, Ewan.

EWAN         I said –

GAVIN        Sing a song.

EWAN         No.

GAVIN        Your public expects, we're waiting, Ewan.

EWAN         No.

GAVIN        Yes, Ewan, yes, come on, seize the moment,
             Ewan.

EWAN         How many times do I have to tell you? My
             name . . .

GAVIN        Sing the song, Ewan.

             (EWAN *starts to sing 'Any Dream Will Do' from
             'Joseph'. He is unsure of himself, vulnerable.*)

GAVIN        Oh, Ewan. That is so gorgeous.

(GAVIN *looks on.*)

GAVIN        That is beautiful.

             (*It quite obviously isn't.*)

GAVIN        That is transcendent, Ewan. I'm getting
             goosebumps.

             (GAVIN *moves towards him, yanks down his
             trousers, and proceeds to bugger him.*)

GAVIN        That's it, Ewan, keep going. Sing, Ewan. Sing
             for fucking Scotland.

             (EWAN *carries on singing, in between the
             thrusts.*)

GAVIN        That's it, Ewan. That's sublime. You are a diva,
             Ewan. Let nobody ever say you aren't, because
             that's what you are, Ewan, a lovely fucking
             diva.


                          Scene Nine

NATASHA *and* DANNY. *They are rehearsing their lines in a
domestic space.* DANNY *still has to tell* NATASHA *what he's
done. They know their lines, but have their scripts nearby.*

NATASHA      'What are you doing?'

DANNY        'Nothing.'

NATASHA      'You keep avoiding me.'

DANNY        'No I don't.'

NATASHA      'Where were you the other night?'

             (*Beat.*)

DANNY        'It's just, something's happened.'

NATASHA      Are you alright?

DANNY       What?

NATASHA     You seem a bit edgy?

DANNY       Do I?

NATASHA     Yea.

            (NATASHA *looks at him.*)

DANNY       What? What is it?

NATASHA     I don't know, Danny, you tell me.

DANNY       Tell you what?

NATASHA     Whatever it is that's . . .

DANNY       Look, look, it's nothing, let's do this, I want to
            do this.

            (*Beat.*)

NATASHA     'You keep avoiding me.'

DANNY       'No I don't.'

NATASHA     'Where were you the other night?'

DANNY       'It's just, something's happened.'

NATASHA     'What do you mean?'

DANNY       'I think we should end it.'

            (DANNY *reacts, obvious distress.*)

NATASHA     Danny?

DANNY       No, it's okay, I'm fine.

NATASHA     What on earth is going on?

DANNY       It's just, I don't know, it must have been
            something I've eaten.

NATASHA        What?

DANNY          Look, let's do this, I want to do the lines.

NATASHA        Is it me?

DANNY          What?

NATASHA        Have I done something?

DANNY          No, no, of course you haven't.

NATASHA        Be honest with me, Danny.

DANNY          I am being honest, it's not you, it's me, that is
               the truth. Believe me, Tash.

               (*Beat.*)

NATASHA        'I knew this was going to happen.'

DANNY          Is that the line, or is that . . .

NATASHA        Danny!

DANNY          Sorry, fuck, of course, sorry, I'm not, say it
               again.

               (*Beat.*)

DANNY          Say it again, Tash. Say the line again.

               (*They are looking at each other. Intense.*)

NATASHA        'I knew this was going to happen.'

DANNY          'Why are you saying that?'

NATASHA        'I had a dream like this. Not this exactly, but I
               knew that what it meant was that it was the end
               for us. And in this dream, you came into my
               bedroom, and you were holding this cardboard
               box, and you said . . .

(*During this speech,* DANNY *has been running things through his head. Suddenly he says, as though to himself.*)

DANNY        Look, Tash . . .

NATASHA      What?

DANNY        Eh?

NATASHA      You just said my name.

DANNY        Did I?

NATASHA      Yes.

DANNY        Why did I do that?

NATASHA      I have no idea, that's why.

DANNY        Jesus, what am I doing, okay, okay, forget I did
             that, that wasn't, I didn't mean to do that.

NATASHA      Because this is important, Danny.

DANNY        Absolutely.

NATASHA      We're not playing at it. It's not a hobby.

DANNY        No, fuck me, of course not, no. No way.

             (*Beat.*)

DANNY        I'm sorry. Carry on. Go for it.

             (*Beat.*)

NATASHA      'And you said, open it. And so I did. And,
             inside, I couldn't quite make it out at first, but,
             it looked like a small animal, but I wasn't sure,
             and so I reached down, and there was this
             thing, with fur, and teeth, and so I picked it up,
             but as I did that, it let out this weird, awful
             noise.'

             (DANNY *lets out a weird, awful noise.*)

| | |
|---|---|
| NATASHA | Danny? What are you doing now? |
| DANNY | I'm so sorry, I didn't mean to do that. |
| NATASHA | Because if there is something . . . |
| DANNY | Okay. Okay. There is, look, I have been meaning to, I need to . . . |

(*As* DANNY *is about to tell the truth,* NATASHA *starts crying.*)

| | |
|---|---|
| DANNY | What, what are you doing? Tash, what's going on here? |

(NATASHA *suddenly reaches out, picks something up, and throws it across the space. It smashes.*)

| | |
|---|---|
| DANNY | Hey, hey, Jesus! |
| NATASHA | Fuck! |
| DANNY | What are you doing? |

(*Silence.*)

| | |
|---|---|
| NATASHA | What's happening to me, Danny? |
| DANNY | What do you mean? |
| NATASHA | I feel so, everything seems so, not normal, and just, one minute, everything is so, I feel so, up, and then, now I feel so fake, and crap, and lost, and now you start being all weird on me, and . . . |
| DANNY | Hey, come on. |
| NATASHA | And then last night, I had that dream. |
| DANNY | What dream? |
| NATASHA | The dream, Danny. The thing in the cardboard box, and you giving it to me. |

| | |
|---|---|
| DANNY | Me? |
| NATASHA | Yes, it was exactly the same as . . . |
| DANNY | Yea, but it wasn't me was it? |
| NATASHA | What? |
| DANNY | When I was in your dream, that was the character, it – |
| NATASHA | No, it was you. |
| DANNY | Yea, but what I'm saying – |
| NATASHA | I had the dream Danny. For real. And, I thought . . . what does that mean, does that mean, because if I'm having the same dream as my character – |

(DANNY *holds* NATASHA, *and calms her down.*)

| | |
|---|---|
| DANNY | Hey, it's okay, it's okay. Everything is okay. |

(*He holds her, wipes her face.*)

| | |
|---|---|
| DANNY | Oh Tash, you're, God, you are so amazing. |
| NATASHA | No I'm not. |
| DANNY | Jesus, you're so, beautiful, and, talented, but, Tash, listen, there is something I have to – |

(NATASHA *kisses* DANNY. *Passionate.*)

| | |
|---|---|
| NATASHA | You were saying? |

(NATASHA'S *hand now starts to make its way into* DANNY'S *trousers.*)

| | |
|---|---|
| DANNY | Yea, I, the thing is, Tash. |
| NATASHA | The thing is what, Danny? |
| DANNY | The thing is . . . |

NATASHA        What? What do you want to tell me, Danny?

DANNY          Oh my God, I want you, I really, fucking, want
               you. Oh yes.

               (*An artificial, erect penis reveals itself. They
               both look at it.*)

NATASHA        This one's for free.

               (*Fellatio.*)

DANNY          Oh, what, that is, oh Tash, oh, oh, I love you, I
               love you, Tash.

               (*As the fellatio continues, rising 'bad jazz', a
               stranger, darker mix than previously heard.
               We can see* DANNY *mouthing the words 'I love
               you'. Music gets wilder.*)


                        Scene Ten

DANIELLE, *the artistic director of the theatre, and* GAVIN *enter,
arguing. Music.* NATASHA *and* DANNY *exit. Music suddenly cuts
out.*

DANIELLE       Gavin, please, I want us . . .

GAVIN          No, no, this is nothing to do with you.

DANIELLE       We have to discuss this.

GAVIN          These are artistic decisions.

DANIELLE       And if you just storm off every time I try to . . .

GAVIN          It is none of your fucking business.

DANIELLE       And I would appreciate it if you stopped
               swearing at me.

               (*Beat.*)

DANIELLE        Ultimately anything presented in this theatre, I
                am responsible, and –

GAVIN           Why are we even having this discussion?

DANIELLE        Because I want us to, find a way to, somehow,
                solve this.

GAVIN           You want to censor this play.

DANIELLE        No, that is not true, that is the last thing I
                want.

GAVIN           Oh yea, you say that, but –

DANIELLE        I am trying to explain to you.

GAVIN           But I know your sort, and the way you operate.

DANIELLE        Look, I just think, this one moment in the play,
                it's, there is a real danger that it would just
                dominate everything.

GAVIN           You have a completely separate agenda.

DANIELLE        It's all people would talk about, it would just
                be this play in which somebody, there was oral
                sex.

GAVIN           And you know that, do you?

DANIELLE        No, but that is what would happen.

GAVIN           How do you know that?

DANIELLE        Because.

GAVIN           How? How do you know that?

DANIELLE        Do I really have to explain?

GAVIN           How do you know that?

DANIELLE        Because it's illegal, isn't it.

GAVIN           What is?

DANIELLE        An erect penis.

GAVIN           An erect penis is illegal?

DANIELLE        Yes. No. Of course, I don't mean.

GAVIN           Because, fuck me, it would take a police state
                and a half to keep an eye on that one.

DANIELLE        Look Gavin, I understand that this moment is,
                it's integral to what you want the play to say,
                and that you want to challenge the audience.

GAVIN           And now you're telling me what I think.

DANIELLE        So we thought there might be a way round this.

                (DANIELLE *fetches out a fake erect penis as
                seen previously.*)

GAVIN           What the fuck is that?

                (DANNY *enters, self-absorbed, a mess.*)

DANNY           Have you seen Tash?

GAVIN           What?

DANNY           Tash? Have you seen her?

GAVIN           No.

DANNY           She's not here?

GAVIN           No Danny, she is not here.

                (DANNY *exits. He doesn't notice the fake erect
                penis.*)

GAVIN           That is fucking ludicrous.

DANIELLE        Why not?

GAVIN           Because, look at it, it's a fake.

DANIELLE        But it's incredibly lifelike. Look, you strap it on like this.

GAVIN           No.

DANIELLE        I'm sure it could work.

GAVIN           I do not believe this is happening.

DANIELLE        It could be a comment, a statement of some sort.

GAVIN           What sort of statement?

DANIELLE        Well, you know, something to do with the essential artifice of the theatrical experience.

GAVIN           Jesus Christ.

DANIELLE        Look, could you tell if that was real or not? Especially if you lit it right.

GAVIN           Don't take this personally.

DANIELLE        What do you think?

GAVIN           But you are a fucking idiot.

                (*Beat.*)

DANIELLE        I'm sorry Gavin, but you cannot do this.

GAVIN           What?

DANIELLE        I'm sorry, but it is too extreme.

GAVIN           It's, what? Define extreme.

DANIELLE        I don't need to define anything, I've just explained that –

GAVIN           You want to know what extreme is? Raping children, now that –

DANIELLE        Of course, yes, I know.

GAVIN        Walking on to a tube train, and blowing
             yourself up is –

DANIELLE     Is extreme, of course.

GAVIN        Dropping bombs on innocent people, now that
             is what I might define –

DANIELLE     Yes, okay, okay, I hear what you're saying.

GAVIN        Christ, I expected there to be some, knee-jerk
             shit hitting the fan somewhere along the line,
             but, fuck me, I was not expecting to come up
             against this sort of, Orwellian, Stalinist
             conspiracy.

DANIELLE     Stalin? Did you just equate me to Stalin?

GAVIN        Same old liberal bullshit.

DANIELLE     What? Objecting to being compared to Stalin?

             (NATASHA *enters dressed as her character, a
             street prostitute.*)

NATASHA      Was Danny here?

GAVIN        Yes.

NATASHA      Was he looking for me?

GAVIN        Yes

NATASHA      And what did you say?

GAVIN        I don't know, he just came in, and fucked off.

             (NATASHA *exits.*)

DANIELLE     Okay, look, I know you have this reputation of,
             being this, this difficult, maverick, genius, and
             I know that working here, it's no doubt
             something of a come down, you know, because

of what you've done in the past, and obviously 'The Changeling'.

GAVIN     Fuck's sake.

DANIELLE     That was such a visceral, seminal production.

GAVIN     And your point is, what exactly?

(DANNY *enters*.)

DANNY     Was she just here?

GAVIN     What?

DANNY     Tash. She was just here wasn't she? Where did she go?

GAVIN     I don't know.

(DANNY *exits*.)

DANIELLE     So, are you saying that anything is permissible?

GAVIN     No, all I'm saying is that if you describe something as extreme –

DANIELLE     I suppose you want people to walk out.

GAVIN     I don't care.

DANIELLE     You don't care if people walk out?

GAVIN     At least they might feel alive for once in their sad fucking lives.

DANIELLE     I find that quite extraordinary.

GAVIN     For fuck's sake, all we're talking about here is a blowjob.

DANIELLE     I don't think there's any point in carrying on with this.

| GAVIN | Because, I mean, it's not as if we've got somebody standing up here mouthing off about Islam have we? Because, now, what about that? |
|---|---|
| DANIELLE | No Gavin, I really do not want to pursue this. |
| GAVIN | Allah, what is the worst thing you could possibly say? |
| DANIELLE | Please, do not, do not even joke about it. |
| GAVIN | Hey, believe me, I am not joking. |
| DANIELLE | Because you cannot say anything like that in a play. |
| GAVIN | Why not? |
| DANIELLE | Because, we, we'd have death-threats, and firebombs, and Christ knows what. |
| GAVIN | But Danielle, think of the publicity. |
| DANIELLE | I was warned about you. |
| GAVIN | What? |
| DANIELLE | When I said to someone you were coming here to direct something, they said – |
| GAVIN | Who? |
| DANIELLE | Someone. |
| GAVIN | Who? Who the fuck was it? |
| DANIELLE | An actor, someone, apparently he was going to be involved in some venture of yours in, in Germany, but then you fell out with the man who was putting up the money, and he said – |
| GAVIN | That is wrong. |
| DANIELLE | He predicted something like this would happen, and I know you've had your problems. |

GAVIN        That is a lie.

DANIELLE     And I'm a great believer in giving someone
             another chance.

GAVIN        You want to get your facts straight, love.

DANIELLE     But if you carry on like this, you leave me with
             no choice.

GAVIN        To do what?

DANIELLE     I have no desire to, but –

GAVIN        You will do what?

DANIELLE     I'll cancel the show, Gavin. If you force me, I
             will. I'll do it.

             (*A standoff.*)

DANIELLE     I'll leave it with you.

             (DANIELLE *exits.* GAVIN *stands.* DANNY *enters.*)

DANNY        Has she been back?

             (GAVIN *does not respond.*)

DANNY        Gavin? Tash? Has she been here since . . .

             (GAVIN *holds up his hand.* DANNY *stops.* GAVIN
             *goes deep into himself. He is obviously
             battling off losing it. A very strange moment.
             He turns and looks at* DANNY.)

GAVIN        Don't go anywhere.

             (*He exits.* DANNY *watches.* NATASHA *enters.*
             DANNY *turns, and sees her. They stare at each
             other.*)

DANNY        Ah. There you are.

             (NATASHA *stares at him.*)

DANNY          Are you okay?

NATASHA        Why?

DANNY          It's just, I was a bit concerned.

NATASHA        Don't be.

DANNY          Because after I left you the other night, you
               seemed . . .

NATASHA        What? I seemed what, Danny?

               (*Beat.*)

DANNY          Look, I understand right, if you're seriously
               pissed off with me, because, I do realise that
               maybe when I told you, you know, about all
               the, the Saskia, baby, thing, I could have
               probably chosen a better moment, and if you
               hate me, I just want to say, I think that's okay,
               although if it makes you feel any better, I feel
               pretty shit myself, although probably nothing
               compared to what you're feeling at the moment.

NATASHA        How do you know how I'm feeling?

DANNY          I don't.

NATASHA        Well don't say you do.

DANNY          I didn't, I said . . .

NATASHA        You did.

DANNY          Alright, if I did, I didn't mean to, but I didn't.

               (*The* STAGE MANAGER *enters.*)

STAGE M        Here, who wants these?

DANNY          What have you got?

STAGE M        I've got one knife, and one syringe.

| DANNY | Thanks, I'll take them. |
| STAGE M | You carry on, I'm just going to bring in the dead dog. |

(STAGE MANAGER *exits.*)

| DANNY | So, where were you last night? |
| NATASHA | Why? |
| DANNY | Because, well, I called round, because, and, I was wondering why, why you weren't in. |
| NATASHA | I was out. |
| DANNY | I know. |

(STAGE MANAGER *enters, carrying a dead dog. He proceeds to watch the following exchange.*)

| DANNY | You were out all night. |

(NATASHA *looks at* DANNY *with some hatred.*)

| DANNY | It's just, I couldn't help noticing that, you, you didn't come home. At all. All night. |

(DANNY *notices* NATASHA *is wearing her costume.*)

| DANNY | Are we supposed to be wearing our costumes? |
| NATASHA | You're sick. I could get you arrested. |
| DANNY | What? |
| NATASHA | I could get you locked up. Harassment. |
| DANNY | No, hey, bloody hell, I just thought we needed to talk. |
| NATASHA | We needed to talk? What about? |
| DANNY | Well, I suppose, it's going to be a bit awkward, isn't it. |

| | |
|---|---|
| NATASHA | We're making a play, Danny. |
| DANNY | I know, I know. |
| NATASHA | That's what is important here. |
| | (DANNY *thinks he might have heard this before.*) |
| NATASHA | Awkward doesn't come into it. |
| DANNY | No, sure, but all I'm saying is, I'm worried about you. |
| NATASHA | Don't be. |
| DANNY | You know, because I've hurt so much. |
| NATASHA | You haven't hurt me Danny, you've helped me. |
| DANNY | Eh? |
| NATASHA | In fact I think I should thank you. |
| DANNY | Why would you want to do that? |
| NATASHA | Thank you, Danny. |
| DANNY | Tash, can I just ask, why are you wearing your costume? |
| NATASHA | Because I'm not playing at it. |
| DANNY | You're not playing at what? What do you mean? |
| NATASHA | Well, what do you think it means? |
| DANNY | You, sorry, you don't, you can't possibly mean . . . |
| NATASHA | Like you said Danny, it's better than waiting. |
| | (DANNY *tries to figure this out.*) |

DANNY        No, no, no, come on, that's not, cut it out,
             please, you don't mean, Tash, because, when,
             when you say, you're not seriously, I mean,
             that is not, no, no, no, no, fuck off, please, no,
             no. No.

             (STAGE MANAGER *applauds*.)

STAGE M      Hey, very good, that. A bit weird but I like it.
             Okay, there you go, one dead dog.

             (*He holds up the dead dog prop. They both
             look at it. Loud rock music. The scene
             suddenly shifts.*)


                        Scene Eleven

*Music cuts out. The technical rehearsal. A screaming match
between the two characters in the play. The dead dog lies
between them.*

NATASHA      'You killed him.'

DANNY        'No, don't say that.'

NATASHA      'You fed him drugs.'

DANNY        'No, no I didn't.'

NATASHA      'You liar.'

DANNY        'He was hungry, I just gave him some food.'

NATASHA      'You killed him.'

DANNY        'Where are my drugs?'

NATASHA      'You killed him, like you kill everything.'

DANNY        'Have you hidden my drugs.'

NATASHA      'Murderer.'

DANNY        'Where are my drugs?'

NATASHA       'I don't know, liar.'

DANNY         'I'm not lying.'

NATASHA       'Liar, liar, liar, liar.'

DANNY         'Shut up.'

NATASHA       'Your life is one big fat fucking lie.'

              (*Very loud rock music.* DANNY *leaps towards*
              NATASHA. *Some choreographed fight moves.*
              *The dead dog is in the way.* GAVIN *steps into*
              *the space. He wears headphones, through*
              *which he is communicating with Joe, the*
              *lighting operator.*)

GAVIN         No. No. Joe. Oi. Cut it.

              (*The music cuts out.*)

GAVIN         Okay, that's not loud enough. Yes, I want it
              louder than that. Yes. No, don't worry about
              that. Just play me the . . .

              (*Loud rock music.* GAVIN *signals for it to stop.*
              *After a moment, it does.*)

GAVIN         Okay. Do that again.

DANNY         That is really loud.

GAVIN         Alright, go from . . .

NATASHA       'Liar, liar, liar, liar.'

GAVIN         (*headphones*) The speakers will be fine.

DANNY         'Shut up.'

              (NATASHA *carries on saying 'liar'.*)

NATASHA       'Liar, liar, liar, liar, liar' (*Etc.*)

DANNY         'Shut up. Shut up.' Look, I've said the line.

NATASHA        'Your life is one big fat fucking lie.'

               (*Music blasts in.* NATASHA *starts the fight
               sequence.* DANNY *is taken by surprise. The
               dead dog is getting in the way again.* GAVIN
               *steps into the space. Gesticulates at the
               lighting box.*)

GAVIN          Oi. Cut. I said. Cut.

               (*Music cuts out.*)

DANNY          I'm sorry, but I said the line, and . . .

GAVIN          What were you doing?

DANNY          No, it's just I thought we'd agreed there'd be
               four liars, and . . .

GAVIN          Go with it, whatever happens, happens.

DANNY          No, sure.

GAVIN          You have to be alive to the moment.

DANNY          No, absolutely, I'm sorry.

GAVIN          Okay Joe, I want to do that again.

DANNY          But Gavin . . .

GAVIN          Yes, now.

DANNY          Gavin?

GAVIN          What? What is it?

DANNY          It's just, I'm not, but the music, it's so fucking
               loud.

GAVIN          (*headphone*) No, when they do the lines.

DANNY          Because, what do you think?

NATASHA        I like it.

GAVIN        Danny, if I want your opinion, I'll ask for it.

DANNY        It's just, all I'm saying is, I think that maybe,
             the music, it's, a bit . . .

             (*Music blasts in.* GAVIN *signals wildly at the
             lighting box. Music cuts out.*)

DANNY        Too loud.

GAVIN        Again.

             (*The actors move back into position.* NATASHA
             *looks at* DANNY *with real hatred. She starts
             soft, and then builds.*)

NATASHA      'Liar, liar, liar, liar, liar. . . '

             (*She carries on saying it.* DANNY *doesn't
             respond, taking the accusation.*)

GAVIN        Oi, are you going to say the fucking line or
             what?

DANNY        Well I'm being alive to the fucking moment,
             aren't I?

NATASHA      'Liar, liar, liar, liar, liar . . . '

             (NATASHA *is now shouting it directly in*
             DANNY's *face.*)

DANNY        Shut up. Shut up. Please, shut up!

GAVIN        (*headphone*) No, wait for the line.

NATASHA      'Liar, liar, liar, liar, liar.'

             (NATASHA *finishes.* DANNY *doesn't say
             anything. Intense.*)

GAVIN        (*headphone*) No, I said wait until . . .

(*The music blasts in.* NATASHA *goes for* DANNY *with violent abandon.* DANNY *struggles to restrain her. She slaps him. It should look as though it really hurts. Things break down badly. Arguing. The music cuts out.*)

DANNY     What the fuck was that? Jesus.

NATASHA   What?

GAVIN     Joe, what are you doing?

DANNY     That really, really hurt. Shit.

GAVIN     I want to do it again. Yes. Wait for the line.

DANNY     Jesus Christ, have I got a mark? I bet I get a fucking bruise.

GAVIN     Do not ask me that again.

NATASHA   Gavin?

GAVIN     I don't care mate, we're doing this until we get it done.

NATASHA   What about if I spit at him?

DANNY     What?

NATASHA   I think it would give you a bit more to react against .

GAVIN     Yea, okay, if you want.

DANNY     No, honestly, I've got enough, I really am fine with what I've got already.

GAVIN     Joe? Let's go.

DANNY     Look, Tash please, don't spit at me.

GAVIN     What? Well, find it.

| | |
|---|---|
| DANNY | Please, I would really prefer it if there was no spitting. |
| GAVIN | It's the second track. |
| NATASHA | So, whatever happened to 'I think actors shouldn't be afraid of pushing themselves to the limits of their possibilities.' |
| DANNY | What? No, I never said that. |
| NATASHA | I heard you say it. |
| DANNY | No, you said it, you said it, Tash. |
| NATASHA | You said it, Danny. |
| DANNY | Look . . . |
| NATASHA | You are such a liar. |
| DANNY | No, no. |
| NATASHA | Liar. |
| DANNY | No, stop it. |
| NATASHA | Your life is one big fat lie. |

(*The music blasts in. It is 'bad jazz'.* GAVIN *signals wildly for it to stop. The music eventually cuts out. Everybody is shouting over each other. Can be slightly improvised.*)

| | |
|---|---|
| DANNY | I am not a liar. |
| NATASHA | What? Did you just say you weren't a liar? Is that what you just said? Is that really what you just said? Danny is not a liar. Now there's a lie to start with. |
| DANNY | Yes, okay, okay, but I didn't lie, I never, technically, I didn't lie. I just never told the whole truth. And there is a difference, I know you might say that that's still a lie. |

GAVIN          No, that was the wrong music, yes, look, I
               know what the fucking music sounds like, no,
               not like that, that's the end of the next scene,
               no, no, you can have a fag when, no, when
               we've finished. Oi, you two, shut up. And you.

               (*Silence.*)

GAVIN          Okay. When you're ready.

               (*Natasha starts.*)

NATASHA        'Liar, liar, liar, liar . . .'

               (NATASHA *repeats 'liar' endlessly.*)

DANNY          Look, Tash, I don't want you to spit in my face.
               Please. Do you hear me?

GAVIN          (*headphone*) No. I don't care.

NATASHA        'Liar, liar, liar, liar . . .'

DANNY          Honestly, I do not want you to spit in my face.

               (*She carries on.*)

DANNY          Please, just shut up.

NATASHA        'Your whole life is one big fat lie.'

               (NATASHA *spits in* DANNY'S *face.*)

GAVIN          I don't believe it, that's the cue, where's the . . .

               (*The music blasts in. If possible, it is even
               louder.* NATASHA *and* DANNY *fight, this time out
               of control completely. The dog gets ruthlessly
               kicked about. They crash into something. The
               music cuts out.* GAVIN *looks very near to
               breaking point.*)

DANNY          I asked you, I even said please, I said, please
               do not spit in my face.

GAVIN           Joe? Joe? Where, oi? Oi. Can you hear me? I
                want to do it again. Fuck.

                (GAVIN *realises Joe has gone for a fag, or*
                *possibly, for good.* GAVIN *holds his head in his*
                *hands. He is in a strange and dangerous*
                *place.*)

DANNY           Gavin?

                (GAVIN *does not respond.*)

DANNY           Gavin?

GAVIN           What?

                (*A piece of the set falls down. It makes a huge,*
                *discordant sound. They all look at it.* GAVIN
                *exits.* DANNY *and* NATASHA *are left with each*
                *other.*)

NATASHA         So? Do you want to rehearse?

                (*Silence.*)

NATASHA         We could do the bit where I suck your penis,
                and then I tell you that I love you.

DANNY           No thanks.

                (*Beat.*)

NATASHA         Liar.

                (NATASHA *exits.* DANNY *is alone.*)


                            Scene Twelve

*Scene bleeds from one to the other. We hear* EWAN'S *voice*
*before we see him.*

EWAN            Hey Danny. Danny? Danny.

(GAVIN *has entered. He is returning home.*)

EWAN     Hey Danny, what's the rush?

(GAVIN *stops. Turns to face.*)

EWAN     How's it going?

GAVIN    What do you want?

EWAN     Hey, what's with the attitude? I just thought
         I'd drop by, you know, see what's what.

GAVIN    Look, I want you to fuck off.

EWAN     Or what?

GAVIN    I haven't got time for this.

EWAN     It's just I  thought I cold sense an 'or what'.
         You know, I want you to fuck off, or I'll be
         doing the following.

GAVIN    No, just fuck off, that's all.

EWAN     Oh, but what if I don't want to do that? What if
         I don't want to fuck off? Eh Gavin?

(*The use of his name stops* GAVIN *from leaving.*)

EWAN     I assume you won't be phoning the police.

GAVIN    What do you want?

EWAN     I want you to read my play.

GAVIN    What?

EWAN     I want you to read my play, and give me some
         constructive feedback.

(EWAN *has taken out a bundle of handwritten
pages, and holds them out.*)

GAVIN    Are you serious?

EWAN            Of course I'm serious Gavin, I'm deadly fucking
                serious.

                (*Beat.*)

EWAN            I think the least you could do is give me a few
                minutes out of your busy schedule.

                (GAVIN *considers, and then signals for* EWAN *to
                pass him the scrappy bits of paper.* GAVIN
                *starts reading.* EWAN *waits.* GAVIN *finishes
                reading.*)

EWAN            Okay, so what do you think?

GAVIN           What do I think?

EWAN            Aye.

GAVIN           I think it's shit.

EWAN            You what?

GAVIN           And that's me being kind.

EWAN            No, no, Gavin, I don't think you understand.

GAVIN           It's illiterate, incoherent, self-pitying drivel.

                (GAVIN *holds out the pages for* EWAN *to take
                them back.*)

EWAN            Is that it? Is that all you've got to say about
                my play?

GAVIN           Aye Ewan, that's my penny's worth.

EWAN            I said I wanted constructive feedback.

GAVIN           Look, do you want it?

EWAN            And I don't think that what you've just said is
                very constructive.

GAVIN      Do you want your play back?

EWAN       Read it again.

GAVIN      What? No.

EWAN       I want you to read it again.

GAVIN      No.

EWAN       Look, I want you to read it again. Do you hear
           me Gavin? I want you to pick up my play, and . . .

GAVIN      No!

           (GAVIN *throws the play down between them.*)

EWAN       You made me sing Andrew Lloyd-Webber and
           fucked me up the arse, and now you're telling
           me my play is shite. Who the fuck do you think
           you are?

           (EWAN *stares at* GAVIN.)

EWAN       Eh? Who the fuck do you think you are?

GAVIN      Go away.

           (EWAN *produces a knife.*)

EWAN       I want you to pick up my play, and say
           something nice about it.

           (*Beat.*)

EWAN       I want some encouragement.

GAVIN      Look Ewan, it is not worth it, all this, this
           artistic, fucking, striving, because, let's say I
           do give you the, the spark of inspiration you
           so desperately crave, eh, and then you trot
           home back to your hovel, and you wrote a play
           that someone wanted to produce, and then lots
           of people came and they told you how deep
           and fucking wonderful you were, even after all

that Ewan, even if you get that, even then, it's still not enough, it still, it doesn't mean anything, because, the thing is Ewan, it's all just a myth built on bullshit.

(*Beat.*)

GAVIN        Now fuck off.

EWAN         That's not encouragement.

(GAVIN *turns away and starts looking for his key.*)

EWAN         What about my play? Gavin? What about my play? I want you to say something about my play.

GAVIN        Look Ewan, forget it, it's not a play, it's just you whinging on about how fucking miserable your life is.

EWAN         Well, it is.

GAVIN        Oh poor little you.

EWAN         I've had a terrible childhood.

GAVIN        So?

EWAN         You are one cruel bastard.

GAVIN        I think you'll find that's a definition of life.

EWAN         I want you to read my play.

GAVIN        Fuck this.

(GAVIN *is very near the end of something. He picks up* EWAN'S *play, and systematically tears it up.*)

GAVIN        My feedback, Ewan.

EWAN         That's my play.

GAVIN            Correction, that was your play.

                 (*They stare at each other.*)

GAVIN            So, Ewan, what happens next?

                 (EWAN *springs forward, and stabs* GAVIN. GAVIN
                 *falls to his knees.* EWAN *drops the knife.*)

EWAN             I spent a whole afternoon writing that. That's
                 my life.

                 (EWAN *starts picking up the remnants of the
                 play, and stuffs them in his pockets.*)

EWAN             You just tore up my life.

                 (EWAN *exits.* GAVIN *is in pain.*)

GAVIN            Play the music.

                 (*Talking almost to himself.*)

GAVIN            Where's the music? I want the . . . now.

                 (*Music. Discordant jazz.*)

GAVIN            Louder. I said, louder. Louder.

                 (*It rises in volume, until we can no longer
                 hear* GAVIN *imploring it to be louder.*)


                          Scene Thirteen

*The music carries on.* DANNY *is preparing to inject himself
with heroin.* HANNAH *enters. She carries a cardboard box.
Music stops abruptly.*

HANNAH           Where is everybody?

DANNY            Hannah? Jesus, what are you doing here?

HANNAH           Where are all the others?

DANNY          I don't know, nobody's turned up.

HANNAH         What are you doing?

DANNY          I was, I'm rehearsing.

               (*Awkward.*)

DANNY          Actually Hannah, now you're here, there was
               something, I, I've been wanting to ask you.
               About the play.

               (HANNAH *looks concerned.*)

DANNY          What does it mean? I know that sounds,
               maybe, a bit thick, because I do understand
               that plays, they're not always so
               straightforward that you go, oh yea, that's
               what they mean, because they're not essays
               are they? I do get that, but do you think you
               could possibly give me a clue, because, what
               are you trying to say? Is there some sort of
               fucking message or what?

               (HANNAH *looks quite frightened at his
               outburst.*)

HANNAH         I don't know. I don't know what it means.

               (DANNY *is crestfallen. Hannah puts down the
               box.*)

DANNY          What's that?

HANNAH         It's for the play.

               (*She exits.* DANNY *looks in the box.*)

DANNY          Holy shit.

               (NATASHA *enters. She looks terrible. Mascara,
               lipstick, all over the place.*)

DANNY          Jesus, what?

NATASHA    Where's Gavin?

DANNY      You look awful.

NATASHA    Danny, I asked you a question.

DANNY      You look really terrible.

NATASHA    Where is Gavin?

DANNY      I don't know where he is. Why should I know
           where Gavin is? Why the fuck would Gavin or
           anybody else tell me, the lowest of the low,
           where he is?

           (*Silence.*)

DANNY      Where have you been, Tash?

NATASHA    What's it to you?

DANNY      Why did you get in that car?

NATASHA    What?

DANNY      I saw you. I saw you in the club, and then you
           got into that car.

NATASHA    Were you stalking me, Danny?

DANNY      Tash, why did you get in that car?

NATASHA    Fuck off, creep.

DANNY      Marry me.

NATASHA    What?

DANNY      Let's get married. What do you think? We
           could get a cottage somewhere, you know, do
           the whole downsize, opt out, go and live in the
           countryside thing. Eh? What do you think? We
           could bake our own bread, and wear jumpers
           that we'd knitted ourselves, and have kids,
           loads of kids, and we'd be fulfilled, because we

wouldn't be trying to achieve stuff. Because, I've had enough, Tash, because if this is what being an actor is like, you can fucking stick it. Just think, we'd wake up and smell nature, and grass, and flowers, and, there'd be birds, and we'd be happy, you know, because I had a three year plan five years ago, and I haven't achieved one thing I set out to. What do you think? And, oh yea, Saskia, you don't have to worry about her, because, we, we decided that it was probably for the best that we, because actually it wasn't my baby. I wasn't the father after all. I know, it turned out it was this other guy, who, he works in computers, well he's got his own company, and, so, yea, it's not my baby, phew, I know, mad, but still, that means, that, we can, what do you think?

(*Silence.*)

NATASHA     So Danny, you want to know where I've been then?

DANNY       Look Tash, the thing is, I've had a big reality check, and . . .

NATASHA     When I got in that car, do you want to know where I ended up?

DANNY       I realised that what we had together, it was totally amazing.

NATASHA     Would you like to know?

DANNY       And I've been a total idiot, and I want us to draw a line under everything that's gone on between us.

NATASHA     Do you?

            (*Beat.*)

NATASHA     We went to this place, a garage, somewhere near the M25.

DANNY          Oh right.

NATASHA        And it turned out it belonged to George.

DANNY          So, sorry, who, who's George?

NATASHA        George is the man I met in the club.

DANNY          Okay.

NATASHA        George is a business man with a quite a diverse
               range of interests.

DANNY          Look, Tash, actually, this isn't important,
               because –

NATASHA        And he, George, when we got there, he said,
               would I like to make a film.

DANNY          A film? What sort of film?

NATASHA        And he said, well, basically, I'd play the central
               character of this young woman whose car has
               broken down, and I get it fixed.

DANNY          You don't mean . . .

NATASHA        By four mechanics.

DANNY          What, so you mean, sorry, there were four
               other actors?

NATASHA        No, they were real mechanics.

DANNY          Okay, look, that's the past, Tash.

NATASHA        Apparently that's the vogue, real men living
               out their fantasies.

DANNY          The important thing is Tash, the important
               thing is, I forgive you, listen to me.

NATASHA        You forgive me?

DANNY        Yes. I forgive you.

NATASHA      You forgive me for going to a garage near the
             M25, and having sex with four different men?

             (DANNY *thinks on this.*)

DANNY        Yes.

NATASHA      I don't need your forgiveness.

DANNY        Okay. If that's what you want, I don't forgive
             you.

NATASHA      It's not a matter of want Danny, that's how it is.

DANNY        No, sure, I respect that, but I was just
             responding to you, when you, you said, look I
             don't know what I'm talking about here, but the
             thing is, Tash, whether you want it or not, I
             forgive you, that's what I'm saying, you know,
             because, you had sex with all of them?

NATASHA      Yes.

DANNY        What, actual –

NATASHA      Yes, Danny.

DANNY        Real –

NATASHA      I think that's how you describe it.

DANNY        Sex?

NATASHA      Yes.

             (DANNY *reels slightly.*)

DANNY        Look, that's okay, I'm, okay with that.

NATASHA      Actual, real.

DANNY        I can deal with that.

NATASHA      Anal sex.

DANNY          What?

NATASHA        I had actual, real –

DANNY          You, what, with four mean?

NATASHA        Yes.

DANNY          You willingly let four men have, anal, sex with you?

NATASHA        Yes.

(DANNY *tries to compute.*)

DANNY          That's alright. I forgive you.

(*They stare at each other.*)

DANNY          Christ al-fucking-mighty!

NATASHA        What's the matter?

DANNY          I mean, fucking hell, didn't it hurt?

NATASHA        A bit.

DANNY          A bit?

NATASHA        But actually, Danny –

DANNY          What?

NATASHA        It was a mind blowing turn on of a night out.

DANNY          Oh no, no, no, no, no, no, don't say that.

NATASHA        Why not?

DANNY          Because, that is not funny.

NATASHA        I never said it was funny, Danny, I said –

DANNY          Yes, okay, I heard you, I know what you said.

| | |
|---|---|
| NATASHA | But the thing is Danny, do you still forgive me? |
| DANNY | Yes. |
| NATASHA | You still forgive me? |
| DANNY | Yes. Yes. I forgive you. |
| NATASHA | But imagine it, Danny. |
| DANNY | Look, Tash, how many times do I have to – |
| NATASHA | Although actually I'm sure I can get you a copy. |
| DANNY | I forgive you. |
| NATASHA | And you'll be able to see for yourself. |
| DANNY | Look, whatever you've done, Tash, you did, and – |
| NATASHA | One up my cunt, one up my arse. |
| DANNY | I'm going to forgive it. |
| NATASHA | A blowjob and a wank, all at the same time. |
| DANNY | We just move on. |
| NATASHA | And if you think about it, that is quite a logistical operation. |
| DANNY | Because I forgive you. |
| NATASHA | And then all of them came over my face. |
| DANNY | Fucking hell! You disgusting filthy sordid bitch whore. |
| | (*Silence.*) |
| NATASHA | So Danny, do you still forgive me? |

(DANNY *is devastated. He takes out the syringe we saw previously. He begins to try and inject himself again.*)

NATASHA    What's that?

(*He is desperately searching for a vein.*)

NATASHA    Danny? What are you doing?

DANNY      What the fuck is it to you? Ow. Bollocks.

(*It hurts.*)

DANNY      Ow. Shit.

NATASHA    Is that really, how did you . . .

DANNY      I'm going show you, ow. Jesus Christ.

NATASHA    You pathetic wanker, you can't even manage to do that.

DANNY      Bloody hell. Ow.

NATASHA    Look, stop it, give it here.

(*She goes to take the syringe off him, but he holds it up to threaten her.*)

DANNY      Hey, hey, get off. You stay away. I'm going to, fucking, do this, okay, because, you're not the only one who can live on the edge, you know.

(DANNY *holds the needle to his arm.*)

NATASHA    Go on then.

DANNY      I am. I'm going to do it. You watch.

(GAVIN *enters, holding himself. Neither of them notice him.*)

NATASHA    Come on then Danny, live on the edge.

(DANNY *is in some psychic pain.*)

DANNY I don't feel right. It's my head, it's full of all
this weird noise I can't get rid of. All these mad
notes, and squeals, and screeches, it's like
some sort of terrible music lodged in my brain. I
feel as if I'm going insane.

(*He is struggling.*)

DANNY What's the next line? I know it, mad notes,
squeals, all that, like some sort of, of terrible
music, lodged in my brain, I feel, as if, I feel as
if I'm going insane. Shit. I feel as if I'm going
insane. I feel as if, as, shit, what's the next
line?

(GAVIN *knocks something over. They turn and
see him. He doesn't look very well.*)

NATASHA Gavin? Are you alright?

(GAVIN *gets back up.*)

GAVIN Okay.

NATASHA Because you don't look very well.

GAVIN Let's do this.

NATASHA Gavin?

GAVIN Look, I'm fine, I am alright, it is not an issue, I
am perfectly okay.

(GAVIN *falls to his knees, in very obvious pain.*
NATASHA *moves towards him.*)

GAVIN Get off. I said, did you hear what I said? Okay,
where were we?

(GAVIN *climbs back up.* DANNY *starts to cry.*)

GAVIN What's he doing?

NATASHA        Nothing. He's nervous.

GAVIN          Oi. Oi. Cut that out. Oi.

DANNY          Hey, get off me, you tosser, leave me alone.

               (GAVIN *notices the cardboard box left there by*
               HANNAH.)

GAVIN          What's this?

               (*He produces a dead dog. More impressive*
               *than the last.*)

GAVIN          How many fucking dead dogs do we have in
               this play?

               (GAVIN *is wracked with pain.* NATASHA *moves*
               *to help him. The dead dog gets kicked about.*)

NATASHA        Gavin, I think you should sit down.

GAVIN          No, no, sod that, I want to do the play.

               (*She notices there is blood on his hands.*)

NATASHA        Is that, Gavin, you're bleeding.

GAVIN          Let's do this.

NATASHA        You need to see a doctor.

GAVIN          Oi, now, come on. When he's dying, that
               moment, now.

NATASHA        Why are you bleeding, Gavin?

               (GAVIN *is wracked with pain, and falls to his*
               *knees again.*)

NATASHA        Gavin, we have to get someone to look at you.

GAVIN          No, get off, we have to do this.

NATASHA        We need to call someone. Please, Gavin –

GAVIN | No. We are doing the play. Tash, we are doing the play.

(*Silence.*)

GAVIN | I thought you were different, Tash. I thought you had a spark of something. You weren't like them.

NATASHA | What?

GAVIN | You were different to all the other hypocrites, and mediocrities, and cowards who want their art, all life-affirming, and safe, and wrapped in a nice moral message. Eh?

NATASHA | But . . .

GAVIN | Come on, Tash, this is where you stop playing at it.

(GAVIN *produces the knife that stabbed him. There is blood on it.*)

GAVIN | Here, take this, and do the scene. You've just stabbed him.

(NATASHA *hesitates.*)

GAVIN | Take the knife!

(NATASHA *takes the knife.*)

GAVIN | Now play the scene.

DANNY | 'Do you think there's a God?'

NATASHA | What?

GAVIN | He's doing the scene, Tash.

DANNY | 'Do you think there's a God?'

NATASHA | 'Yes.'

DANNY          'You're only saying that because I'm dying.'

NATASHA        'You are not dying.'

DANNY          'I am, I'm dying.'

GAVIN          I don't believe you.

DANNY          'I am, I'm dying.'

GAVIN          You don't sound like someone who's about to die.

DANNY          'I am, I'm dying.'

GAVIN          I don't believe you!

DANNY          Okay Gavin, show me, why don't you show me, what does somebody about to die sound like?

               (GAVIN *emits a truly terrible, strangulated sound of a man about to die.*)

DANNY          What? I'm not doing that. Fuck this, I'm not doing this anymore, I've had enough.

               (*A member of the audience shouts 'you're not the only one'.* GAVIN *shouts back at them.*)

GAVIN          Oi. Shut it. Know your place, wankers.

DANNY          This is insane.

GAVIN          You fake. You fucking wannabe, amateur, loser.

DANNY          Loser? You're calling me a loser? You need to take a step back, and have a good look, because I'm not the loser, you're the loser, you are the saddest, mad bastard in the pack, mate.

GAVIN          Do the scene.

DANNY          No.

GAVIN        Do the scene.

DANNY        No.

GAVIN        You are not allowed to say no.

             (GAVIN *leaps across and grabs* DANNY *by the
             throat. The loud rock music kicks in. Mayhem.*
             NATASHA *tries to intervene. She picks up the
             syringe, and sticks it into* GAVIN'S *arm. The
             music cuts out.* GAVIN *reels back, the syringe
             still in him.*)

NATASHA      Oh, shit, I didn't mean to . . . Gavin?

             (*They watch, in horror, as* GAVIN *takes hold of
             the syringe, and injects the heroin into his
             arm. He pulls it out, and falls to his knees.
             Three exhausted people.*)

NATASHA      Gavin, please, let me call . . .

GAVIN        No.

             (*They both recognise he is about to die.*)

NATASHA      Gavin? Can you hear me?

             (DANIELLE *enters.* GAVIN *is convulsed with
             pain. He reaches to his stomach, and pulls out
             something red that drips between his fingers.*)

GAVIN        What the fuck is that?

             (DANIELLE *vomits, and exits.*)

GAVIN        Okay. Do the scene.

             (NATASHA *holds* GAVIN *as they say the final
             lines.*)

DANNY        'What do you think Heaven looks like?'

NATASHA      'Heaven? I think Heaven is, it's whatever you
             want it to be. I know that sounds really cheesy,

but, I do think that. Because even if your idea
of Heaven is Hell, that's how it will be.
Because, the important thing is, you belong,
you don't have to be on the outside looking in
anymore.'

GAVIN        Bullshit.

(GAVIN *dies. Applause. Music.*)


Scene Fourteen

NATASHA *and* BEN. *A calm, serene atmosphere, in direct
contrast to previous. A café in a park.* NATASHA *smokes a
cigarette, and drinks a coffee, and nibbles on a cake, whilst*
BEN *sips a juice.* BEN *is incredibly contained in comparison to
the last time we saw him.* NATASHA *has a nervy energy. Silence.*

NATASHA      How's your juice?

BEN          It's good.

             (*Silence.*)

NATASHA      What did you have in the end?

BEN          Carrot and ginger.

NATASHA      Oh right, you didn't go for, the one with, the
             apple, and, that one, with the cinnamon.

BEN          No.

             (*Silence.*)

NATASHA      Are you sure you wouldn't like a piece of this?

BEN          No thanks.

NATASHA      I'm not going to be able to eat it all, here,
             please, have a bit.

BEN          No, honestly, I have enough. Thank you.

(*Silence.*)

NATASHA        So, what, are you, because now that you're
               back, what are you, because, what are you
               going to do with yourself?

BEN            Tash . . .

NATASHA        What?

BEN            Sometimes it's okay to be quiet.

               (NATASHA *is pulled up.*)

BEN            Too often I think we talk for the sake of filling
               the void. It's as if we're programmed to make
               this, noise.

               (*Silence.*)

BEN            And silence is good. Silence is healthy. If
               there's anything I want to carry with me at all
               times from my experience, that's it. Don't be
               afraid of the void.

               (*Beat.*)

NATASHA        Are you telling me off?

BEN            No.

NATASHA        You think I'm talking too much?

BEN            Maybe.

NATASHA        So you are telling me off?

BEN            No.

NATASHA        It sounds like it.

BEN            No, Tash, you may choose to see it as that, but
               I am not telling you off.

(NATASHA *puts out one cigarette, and
immediately lights up another.*)

NATASHA      I feel a bit silly now. Because I don't know if I
             say something, if that's me talking for the sake
             of talking, or, or . . .

BEN          Look, Tash, all I'm attempting to say in my own
             inadequate way, is, I recognised there was this
             deep emptiness at the centre of my experience.
             I was too caught up in the, the trivial, in this
             instant gratification society where we're all
             looking for the next fix, this cultural decadence
             that we're all drowning in.

             (*Silence.*)

NATASHA      So, meditation, I mean, what exactly, when you
             sit there, and you, you just, what? What
             exactly, is it?

BEN          Meditation is the conscious attempt to explore
             the nature of reality.

NATASHA      And so, what's it like?

BEN          What's what like?

NATASHA      Reality.

BEN          It's, this.

             (BEN *indicates everything surrounding them.*)

NATASHA      And, that's, what's that?

BEN          It's reality.

             (NATASHA *is mystified.* BEN *smiles benignly. A
             waiter comes over to their table. It is* DANNY.)

DANNY        Excuse me, have you finished?

NATASHA      Danny.

(DANNY *was not expecting this.*)

DANNY Tash. Hi.

NATASHA Hi.

DANNY Wow. Hi.

NATASHA You remember Ben?

DANNY Yea, of course. Ben. Hi.

NATASHA Ben's been in North Wales the last six weeks, meditating.

DANNY Oh right, nice one. So, what, are you a Buddhist then?

BEN I prefer to think of myself as a human being.

(*Beat.*)

NATASHA So, you're working here then?

DANNY Yea, I am, that's right. It's okay, they're very flexible, you know, if an audition comes up.

NATASHA Oh, what have you been up for?

DANNY Not a lot. Well, nothing actually, but they said, if something did come up, that would be, they'd be fine with that.

(*Beat.*)

DANNY What about you? Anything happening?

NATASHA No, no, not at the moment. Maybe. In time.

DANNY I'm really sorry I didn't speak to you at the funeral.

NATASHA That's okay.

DANNY It was just all a bit weird. And it was my first ever funeral.

| | |
|---|---|
| NATASHA | Yea, me too. |
| DANNY | And I, I'd dropped some acid as well. |
| | (*Beat.*) |
| DANNY | But I noticed you, you were speaking to Hannah? |
| NATASHA | Yes, she, yea, she seemed okay. |
| DANNY | What's she up to? |
| NATASHA | She said she was thinking of doing some voluntary work. |
| DANNY | Okay. |
| NATASHA | Oxfam. |
| DANNY | Oh right, what, she's going to go, to Africa, somewhere like that? |
| NATASHA | No, no, I think was she just thinking of, of working in the shop. |
| | (*Awkward.*) |
| BEN | Life is a mysterious riddle to which we have no answer. |
| | (*Silence.*) |
| DANNY | Do you want anything else? |
| NATASHA | No thank you. No, actually, I have to go. |
| DANNY | Wow, what a coincidence. |
| NATASHA | I know, how weird. |
| | (*Beat.*) |
| DANNY | I don't suppose, I mean, if you're free sometime, maybe we could . . . |

NATASHA          I don't think so. No.

                 (BEN *smiles at* DANNY. DANNY *exits.*)

NATASHA          I think I'm going to make a move.

                 (NATASHA *doesn't move. As the speech
                 progresses, the stage is cleared.*)

NATASHA          My therapist said I should write something
                 about all this. About, you know, everything
                 that's happened, and he said, that way I might
                 make some sense of it. I have been making
                 some notes, nothing tangible, half-thoughts
                 really, nothing that makes any real, although I
                 did start something the other night, because, I,
                 I couldn't sleep, but I threw it away, because,
                 how do you put yourself on stage, how do you
                 write yourself as a character when you're not
                 sure who you are anymore? And Lance, my
                 therapist, he, he said that, the really positive
                 thing about writing about your own experience,
                 if I was to do that, would be that, the really
                 important thing is you get to decide your own
                 ending. You know, like a character in a play.
                 You become the playwright of your own life.
                 Because, actually, this, me sitting here with
                 you, this could be an ending couldn't it?
                 There's a definite, end, feel isn't there? Sort of
                 post everything that's happened, and
                 obviously, somehow, I'd have to bring in a
                 reference to, to Gavin, because, and I haven't
                 told anyone about this, but after the funeral, I
                 took his ashes, well neither of his ex-wives
                 wanted them, and I thought I should do
                 something with them, a ritual, somewhere, so, I,
                 I went to Germany, you know, the factory
                 where, but the thing is, it wasn't there, there
                 was a shopping mall, but how would I show
                 that, or maybe, I'll just do it in a speech where
                 I'm telling someone, and, but the thing is, I
                 wouldn't want the ending to, to be sad, no, not
                 sad, I don't mind sad, I don't want it to be, I

think there should be some light, some, hope, I
know Gavin would, he'd hate it, but I think
when you tell stories, whatever has happened,
there has to be, you need to be able to see a
way through. People like that don't they? I like
that. I think I do. And, I suppose, I could make
a, there could be a long speech, where, you
know, I'm sorting through, my thoughts, a bit
like this, but it would be a speech, and, I'm not
sure if it would work, but, I don't know, it
could somehow, I could start it at the end of
the scene in the park, you know, it might be a
bit odd, but, after you going on about the
nature of reality, and then you could say that
line about, what was it, about drowning in, in . . .

BEN            Cultural decadence.

NATASHA        Yes, your character could say that, and then
Danny could turn up, and it could be like, wow,
that's a coincidence, but it would serve a
dramatic purpose, and then we have that sort
of conversation where you want to say so
much, but you don't say anything, because
actually there's nothing you can say, or you're
not ready, and then, that's when I would start
the speech. (*To* BEN.) Look, will you go. I want
you to leave. I want to be on my own.

(BEN *exits.*)

NATASHA        And then when you've gone, and I'm sitting
there, and it's one of those moments where,
things, you feel as if, things are coming in to
some sort of focus, and, I'd get up, and I'd
start to walk off. I would walk away, and I
would, just, carry on walking. I wouldn't have
any idea where I was headed, but I would, if
you know what I mean, and obviously if it was
a film, you could do it really well, you know
with the camera high up, and me becoming this
small dot in the distance, and there would be
this feeling, that somehow, out of all this, I'm
going to do something, I've reached a place

where I'd be able to, shape all this experience, and turn it, into something, a play, something that would exist, out there, in the world, and then when I've done that, when I've achieved that, I'll be sorted, or, I'll be okay, I will have reached a, for the time being, because, I would be out the other side. I, I'd be me.

(*Empty stage.*)

NATASHA    Or whoever plays me could be me. Does that make sense?

(*Bad jazz.*)

THE END

BAD JAZZ
First published in 2007
by Josef Weinberger Ltd
12-14 Mortimer Street, London, W1T 3JJ
www.josef-weinberger.com
general.info@jwmail.co.uk

ISBN 978 085676 298 7

Printed in England by Commercial Colour Press plc, Hainault, Essex